MW01404787

An Introduction to the Physics of Sports

Vassilios McInnes Spathopoulos

An Introduction to the Physics of Sports
Copyright © 2013 by Vassilios Mcinnes Spathopoulos

All rights reserved. No part of this book may be used or reproduced in any manner whatsoever including Internet usage, without written permission of the author.

Cover design by Jeremy Taylor and Les Denton

Book design by Maureen Cutajar
www.gopublished.com

ISBN-13: 978-1483930077
ISBN-10: 1483930076

*To my friend Anup and the memories
from the 2010 World Cup*

An Introduction to the Physics of Sports

How are Newton's three laws connected to football, and various forms of energy to cycling? What is the relationship between figure skating pirouettes and rotational motion? Do basic aerodynamics concepts influence performance in ski jumping, and hydrodynamics mechanisms, the world records in swimming?

The aim of the author, who is a university lecturer in flight physics, is to present the physical laws that affect various sports. With the help of simple simulations it is easily appreciated that science defines the performance of athletes, whereas at the same time the reader is introduced to basic physics concepts in a novel and pleasant way.

Contents

Introduction		1
Chapter 1:	Incredible speed races	3
Chapter 2:	Newton on the ball	17
Chapter 3:	Rotational motion and impressive pirouettes	33
Chapter 4:	High energy sports	47
Chapter 5:	Various sport projectiles	69
Chapter 6:	Aerodynamics in sport	85
Chapter 7:	Are all records the same?	105
Bibliography		115

Introduction

This book presents the physical mechanisms governing a series of popular sports. The author's goal is twofold: on the one hand to give a new perspective on sport, enabling fans, even those with limited scientific knowledge, to gain a better idea of exactly how athletic performances are achieved. On the other hand, the presentation of the basic concepts of physics through sport is an attractive and popular way for the general public to assimilate these concepts.

In Chapter 1 the concepts of speed and acceleration are presented through the performance of top athletes such as Usain Bolt. In Chapter 2 Newton's three fundamental laws of motion are described with examples from sports such as football and basketball. In Chapter 3, the discus, the gymnastics and the pirouettes of athletes in diving and figure skating are used to illustrate the physical principles that govern rotational motion. In Chapter 4 it is described how the various forms of energy, such as kinetic and potential, are used by athletes to set records in sports such as pole vaulting, cycling etc. In Chapter 5 the theory of projectiles is used to calculate parameters such as optimal launch angle, maximum range, margin of error, etc. for sports including the shot put, long jump, basketball and tennis. In Chapter 6 the basic principles of aerodynamics and hydrodynamics are presented, as well as the way they are applied to sports such as the javelin throw, ski jumping and swimming. Finally, in Chapter 7 an overview is provided of the external factors influencing the performance of athletes, such as weather conditions and altitude, as well as methods that may offer a more objective comparison of records.

In all the chapters, simulations, specially created for the purpose of the book, complement the theoretical concepts. The simulations are based on mathematical models of sports, one of the key research interests of the author.

Chapter 1: Incredible speed races

High speeds and accelerations fascinate most of us. The feeling we get when an airplane takes off or when we start a ride on a roller coaster, is surely unique. In the case of sport, when we are referring to high speed, there is one athlete that immediately comes to mind: Usain Bolt! By carefully analysing his incredible performance, we will understand more about the physics involved in setting his amazing records.

A few thoughts on speed and acceleration

We live at a time when speed rules our lives. Our everyday routines depend on it. Almost all of us that work in big cities feel our alarm clock like the starter pistol initiating our daily schedule. Our first mission is to arrive at our work before our boss shows us a.. yellow card. So if for example we are living somewhere that is 15 minutes by car from our office, what is the speed that we need to be going at in order to avoid the caution from the boss?

The answer to this may look simple but it actually requires a bit of thought. Most of us are aware of the fact that in order to calculate speed, we must divide distance by time. In physics we say that speed is given by the formula,

$$V = \frac{S}{t}$$

Where, S is the distance and t is the time.

If we assume that the road from our home to our office is 7.5 kilometers long, then the answer that comes naturally to mind is that we must drive at a speed of 7.5km/0.25hrs, i.e. 30km/hr. The terms km/hr are the *units* of speed that we have used in this example. As we will see, physicists are often more comfortable with units that we are not used to in our everyday dealings.

If you look of course at the speed indicator, it will rarely show this value, i.e. 30km/hr. Once you are on a high speed road for example, you may reach 70km/hr. On the other hand, as we approach the centre, pedestrians will probably overtake you, while you are stuck at some traffic light.

The key here is the difference between *average* and *instantaneous* speed. The former is found by dividing the *total* distance covered by the *total* time taken. On the other hand, the instantaneous speed (i.e. that shown on the indicator), reveals how fast we are travelling at that specific instant. It also, results as the quotient of distance over time, the difference being that it is not the total time but a very small increment measured at that particular instant. The smaller this time increment is, the closer our result approaches the instantaneous velocity. In physics we say that the time increment *tends* to zero, i.e. becomes as small as possible. So for example, if during our trip to our office we had only used the time we were on the fast lane, we would have calculated a speed value much closer to the instantaneous speed at that moment.

The average speed, as the term implies, can be viewed as an average value of all the instantaneous speeds. Moving to the world of sport, when Usain Bolt broke the 100 meters world record in Berlin, in 2009,

Chapter 1: Incredible speed races

his time was 9.58 seconds. How fast did Bolt run at this race? A first approach would be to estimate his average speed. By subtracting his reaction time, which for that race was 0.146 seconds, we find that the actual time taken to cover the 100 meters was 9.434s (seconds). It follows, that his average speed was 100/9.434, which is 38.15km/hr. So by comparing average speeds, Bolt travelled faster than your car did. Of course the car covered 7.5km, whereas Bolt stopped after 100 meters.

More interestingly though, what was his instantaneous speed during the race? The most accurate method is to use the, so called, split times, i.e. the times taken to cover each 10 meter interval. The following table obtained from the IAAF (International Association of Athletics Federations) can be used for this.[1]

Position (m)	Time (s)	Speed (m/s)
10	1.89	5.73
20	2.88	10.10
30	3.78	11.11
40	4.64	11.63
50	5.47	12.05
60	6.29	12.20
70	7.10	12.35
80	7.92	12.20
90	8.75	12.05
100	9.58	12.05

Table 1.1: Split times of Usain Bolt when he broke the 100m world record

The values in the third column are derived by dividing the 10 meters of each split by the time that is needed to cover it. For example, for the last 10 meters, we find the answer, 10/(9.58-8.75) = 12.05m/s. As the time increments are now much smaller, the speeds that we calcu-

---

[1] See, http://berlin.iaaf.org/mm/document/development/research/05/31/54/ 20090817073528 _httppostedfile_analysis100mmenfinal_bolt_13666.pdf

5

late are closer to the instantaneous speed of the athlete. In reality of course, these are the average speeds for each split. In any case though, they still provide a very useful indication of the athlete's performance. By use of this approach we deduce that the maximum speed is 12.35m/s, just over 44.46km/hr. Bolt may find it difficult competing against your car in the fast lane but he would have a good chance if you were driving a small motorbike. Interestingly, if he managed to maintain this speed throughout the race, he would clock a time of 100/12.35 = 8.1s.[2] This of course would be not possible as his speed is not constant but varies according to the value of his *acceleration*.

The characteristic feeling we get in our stomach when we travel at high speed is not a result of the speed itself, as it is sometimes wrongly believed. In reality, what increases our adrenaline is our *acceleration*, i.e. the variation of speed with time. This can easily be proven as follows. During the takeoff phase of a typical airliner, the aircraft will start of from rest and reach a speed of approximately 250km/hr (i.e. 70m/s) until it lifts off the ground. If you look at your watch (I have done this several times), you will find that the time taken is about 30 seconds. The speed has changed by 70m/s in 30s, so the aircraft is moving with an average acceleration of 70/30 = 2.33m/s^2. For a fighter pilot this acceleration would seem negligible since during certain maneuvers, he/she will experience accelerations much higher than that. Even so, for us, the sensation is quite remarkable, especially if we are flying for the first time.

Before continuing it is worth mentioning the units of acceleration that were given as m/s^2. These units are defined as meters per second squared. A quantity is "squared", when it is multiplied by itself, i.e., 1s^2 = 1s*1s. If it is a number, we simply multiply it by itself, i.e. 8^2 will give us 64.

So what happens during the rest of your flight? If you have the chance to fly in an aircraft with entertainment screens, you'll notice that you are provided with information on the flight details, such as speed, altitude

---

[2] Without taking into account the reaction time.

Chapter 1: Incredible speed races

and temperature that is often more interesting than the movies shown. You will find that after reaching the predetermined altitude, the aircraft will maintain a constant speed of around 800km/hr, more than three times the takeoff speed. Is the feeling you get three times more intense? Probably not, as you are about to fall asleep, because (apart from the slight turbulence), you do not feel much at all. However high it may be the speed is not changing so the acceleration is zero, and the means of adrenaline stimulation remains inactive.

Wrapping up our thoughts on speed and acceleration, imagine you are next to a train, at a station platform, with other trains sitting next to yours. At some point, you look out of the window and are sure that your train is moving. After a few seconds you realise that you are actually still sitting at the platform. What has happened?

The illusion that you had of commencing your trip, is due to what is termed as *relative speed*. To understand this, assume that as you are travelling by car on a fast lane, a police car is moving in the opposite direction, slowly at a speed of 30km/hr (see figure 1.1). At some point the police signal to you to stop and inform you that according to their radar you were travelling at 100km/hr. You insist that your indicator was showing 70km/hr. Who is telling the truth?

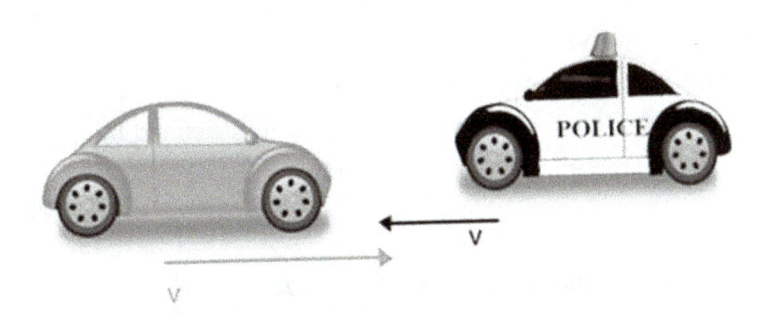

Figure 1.1: Relative speed

7

What has happened is that the relative speed between you and the road is of course 70km/hr. Relative to the police car though that is moving towards you, you are moving with 70+30 = 100km/hr. When two objects are moving in opposite directions, their relative speed is the sum of their individual speeds. When the motion occurs in the same direction, we subtract the two speeds. Your only chance of avoiding a penalty is if the policeman on duty happens to have some knowledge of basic physics.

Returning to the station platform, what has happened is that the train next to yours has started to move, so although relative to the platform you have remained stationary, you have obtained a relative speed in relation to the other train. This has given you the wrong impression that you are moving and that your journey has started earlier than expected.

From figure 1.1, another important fact can be observed. Many physical quantities, apart from the value they take (in physics we call it *magnitude*), also have a certain direction. These quantities are *vector quantities*, and can be represented as arrows. The size of the arrow is proportional to the magnitude of the quantity. In our case, the arrow denoting the motion of the police car is less than half the size of that denoting your motion. The direction of the arrow on the other hand, portrays the direction of the physical quantity. It should be noted that in actual fact, when physicists refer to speed, they are only referring to a magnitude. The associated vector quantity (with a magnitude and a direction) is referred to as the *velocity* of the object. Other vector quantities are force, torque and impulse, more on those in later chapters. Quantities such as mass on the other hand, that can be fully defined by their magnitude, are not vector but *scalar* quantities.

The race of the century: Usain Bolt vs Airplane

As we previously discussed the speed and acceleration performance of an aircraft during takeoff, it would be interesting to see how these compare to the abilities of our athlete. For this, we need to create two mathematical models, in other words a set of equations that represent, at least to a certain degree, the performance of the athlete and of an aircraft during the take off phase. We can then simulate a race in order to find out which of the two, the fastest athlete in the world or one of our greatest technological achievements, will come first.

The mathematical modeling, i.e. deriving the mathematical equations that represent the model, is quite complicated, so I will not go into it in detail. The same applies to the models presented in later chapters of the book. What I should point out, is that for an airplane, I chose the Northop T-38 Talon, twin engine, supersonic, trainer jet. This was the first supersonic trainer and one of the most popular ever, so we are certainly dealing with a tough competitor.[3]

The fastest sprint races are those of the 100 meters and 60 meters. We will compare the performance of the two competitors in both distances. The results are presented in the following figures. The dark line represents the aircraft and the lighter one, Bolt.

At first glance we notice that the two competitors are very close to each other, especially for the 60m. A more detailed analysis reveals that the airplane wins the 100m, by a margin of 1.3s, whereas our athlete wins the 60m by about 0.2s! The representative of the human race starts off impressively and actually leads the race for the first 66m. It is a great achievement in any case, considering that each engine of the T38 produces a huge amount of thrust.

---

[3] Strictly speaking, it should be noted that in the model used, the thrust of the engines is calculated without the use of an afterburner that provides airplanes with extra thrust.

An Introduction To The Physics Of Sports

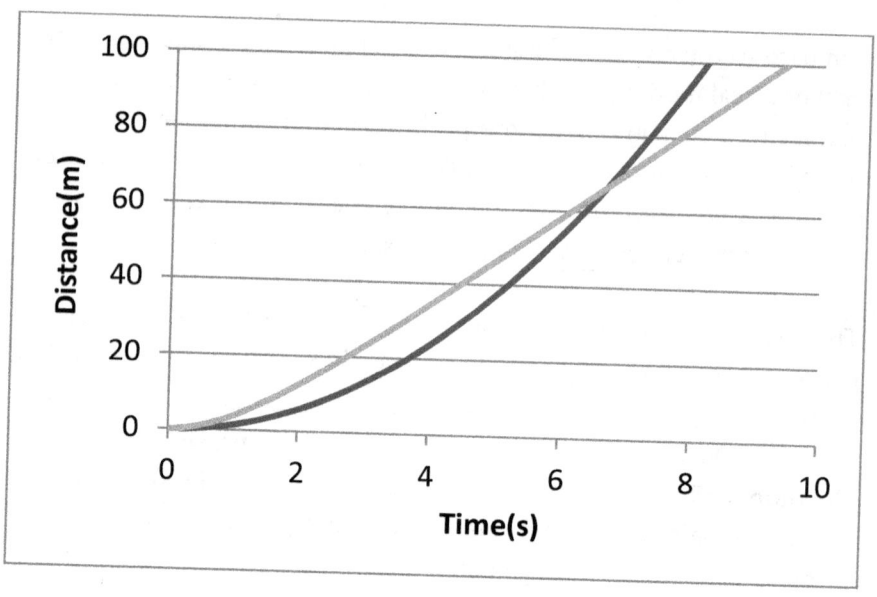

Figure 1.2: Distance comparison

To fully understand what is happening, we need to study the variation of speed and acceleration (see figures 1.3, 1.4).

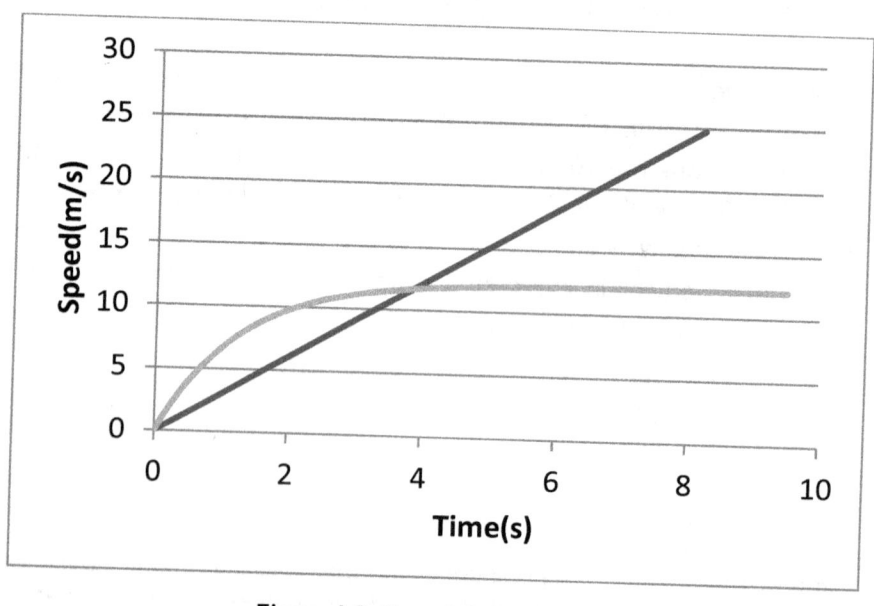

Figure 1.3: Speed Comparison

Chapter 1: Incredible speed races

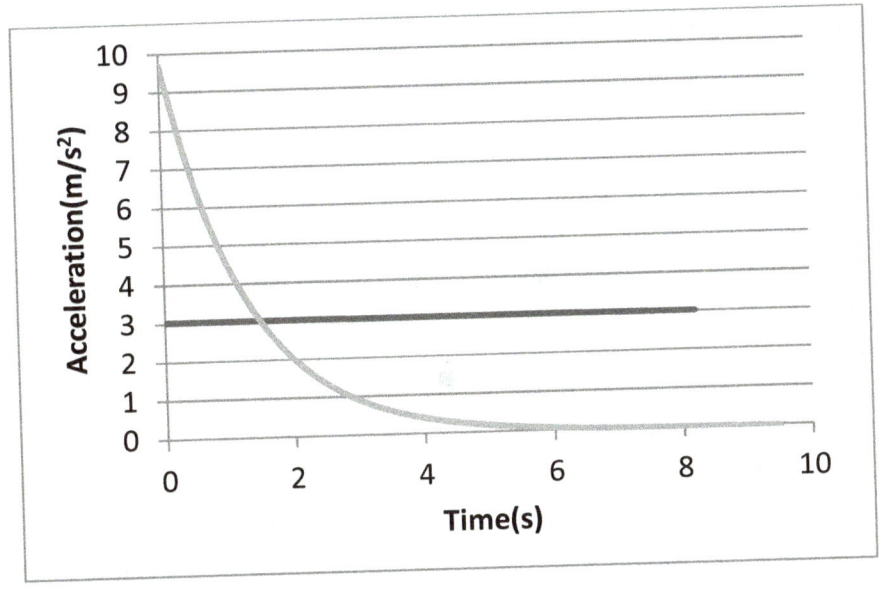

Figure 1.4: Acceleration comparison

From the last figure we can see that the airplane maintains an almost constant acceleration, of just over 3m/s² which drops very slightly due to the presence of air resistance (more about this force later). When we move with a constant acceleration the speed increases at a constant rate, as observed in figure 1.3. The final speed of the airplane after 100m is 24.7m/s, almost 89km/hr.

The above could have been deduced from simple kinematics formulas (the field of physics that deals with this type of problem). If we assume the acceleration (a) of the airplane to be constant at 3m/s², then from physics we know that its speed (V) after time t, is given by the formula,

$$V = at$$

Also the distance covered in time t is,

$$S = \frac{at^2}{2}$$

From this and by use of simple algebra, we can calculate that the 100m are covered by the airplane in 8.16s.

Returning to our race, we see that our athlete makes an explosive start. His initial acceleration is 9.7m/s2. This is almost the acceleration of someone descending freely towards Earth, so he starts off as if falling from the balcony of a high building! Due to his high initial acceleration his speed increases dramatically and reaches 10m/s (36km/hr), in about 2.2s.

Human power though has its limitations and as we see, his speed reaches a maximum that cannot be overcome (just over 12m/s) and, in fact, it falls slightly during the last few meters. In summary, Bolt starts off with a huge acceleration, more than three times that of the airplane, which is enough to win him the 60m section of the race. On the other hand, his acceleration starts to fall immediately and the aircraft, which maintains an almost constant acceleration, wins the 100m.

So according to our calculations, the race between human and airplane ends in a draw. It should be reminded that the mathematical models used, especially that for the airplane, contain many simplifications and the scope of this example was to comprehend certain principles and not necessarily to announce a winner. The same applies to the rest of the simulations used in this book.

At this point, we can take the opportunity to see how humans would favor against other members of the animal kingdom. The following table is quite revealing.

It can be seen that it would not be wise to take on any of the above; Usain Bolt would find it hard to even surpass an elephant. On the other hand, the sight of an elephant running towards you may be enough to make you break the world record.

Chapter 1: Incredible speed races

Animal	Speed (m/s)	Sped (km/hr)
Human	12	43
Cheetah	29	105
Racing horse	25	90
Lion	22	80
Hunting dog	20	72
Cat	13	48
Elephant	11	40

Table 1.2: Speeds of various animals

Does there exist a speed in nature though that cannot be surpassed, an ultimate, maximum speed? According to Einstein's theory of relativity, the answer is yes. The ultimate speed record is held by light, which in a vacuum travels at 300000km/hr. In the time it takes Bolt to complete the 100m, light can cover 3 million kilometers, i.e. the return journey to the moon, four times. If you have watched athletes compete at a stadium, you may have been under the impression that they start their races before the pistol is heard. This is due to the fact that sound travels much more slowly (approximately 340m/s in air), and so it reaches your ears a little later than the image does. This is also why we see lightning before we hear the associated thunder.

When we are discussing impressive runs, It would of course constitute an omission not to mention those runners that, although do not reach high speeds, are able to complete great distances in very quick times. So for example, if we take the current world record for the men's 10000m, it is 26 minutes and 17.53 seconds, i.e. 1577.53s. From this time we obtain an average speed of 10000/1577.53 = 6.34m/s, almost 23km/hr.

If you were to run at this speed, you could cover 100m in just 15s. Most of us would find this time quite hard to achieve. The athletes competing at 10000m, manage to maintain it for a distance 100 times longer.

Zeno's paradox

It is worth finishing off this chapter by mentioning another imaginary race known as "the paradox of Zeno of Elea", an ancient Greek philosopher of the 5th century BC. The story goes like this:

The tortoise challenged Achilles (the Usain Bolt of his time), to a race, boasting that it could beat him as long as it was given a head start of 10m. Achilles of course laughed, thinking that this would be a walk over. The tortoise though, full of confidence, started to prove to him that he was wrong.

"If I start 10m ahead of you, do you think you will reach that point very quickly?"

"Of course, very quickly indeed", Achilles answered.

"How far do you think I will have moved during this time?" it asked again.

"Maybe one meter", Achilles answered after a bit of thought.

"Very well, so there is still a one meter difference between us. You surely believe that you will cover this distance very quickly, don't you?"

"Exactly!"

"Again though, I will have moved slightly ahead, so a difference will still exist between us, is this not the case?"

"This is the case.."

"So you see that every time you reach the point where I was previously, I will have moved on slightly, and there will always exist an, albeit, small distance between us".

Chapter 1: Incredible speed races

"Yes, this is true," replied a disappointed Achilles.

"So you will never be able to reach me and I will have won the race!" said the tortoise triumphantly, offering us hope that we also might be able one day to beat Bolt himself.

This paradox can be redefined as follows. Let us say that we want to go from one side of a room to the opposite one. We will first have to cover half the total distance. After this, once we have reached the midpoint, we will first have to cover the half of the remaining distance, i.e. a quarter of the total distance. Subsequently, when we reach that point, we will again first have to cover half the distance of the remainder, i.e. an eighth of the total distance, etc. This seems to go on forever and as a result we never manage to reach the other side of the room.

The solution to the above paradoxes was provided by mathematical concepts that were developed many centuries after Zeno. What we are actually dealing with is a sum of an infinite series of numbers. By taking for example the second paradox, if the length of the room is 4m, the total distance that we cover is, 2+1+0.5+0.25+0.125+.... Even though the numbers are infinite, it turns out that their sum is not; in this case it is quite obvious that the sum is the 4m that we expect to get. Just don't try crossing your room using Zeno's logic, as you may spend the rest of your life doing so! In a similar way, we can prove that Achilles will of course reach the tortoise. As the tortoise though was much cleverer, history has declared it as the undisputed winner of that race.

15

Week #2 Notes

$S = \frac{1}{2} at^2$ = Constant acceleration

$S = \frac{1}{2}$

Chapter 2: Newton on the ball

It can be said that in terms of popularity, football holds the title of king of sports. It is the medium that unites millions of people around the world, often determining their everyday mood and emotions. It is quite telling that FIFA, the International Federation of Association Football, has 209 members, whereas the United Nations just 193[4][4]. How many of us have not woken up one morning feeling grumpy just because the night before our favorite player missed a crucial penalty kick during an important game? Reading the sports newspapers the next day, we may find out that the reason that the ball did not end up in the net is because the player is not on form, or even more scientifically, that he is just unlucky when he takes crucial penalty kicks for his team.

On the other hand, Newton certainly holds the title of king of classical physics. He was the first to show us that the same physical laws that define the drop of an apple also determine the motion of planets million of kilometers from our Earth; a truly remarkable leap in human knowledge.

How many of us, even those with some scientific knowledge, have thought that the real reason that the ball hit the post, may have more

---

4 Football associations such as that of Scotland, Wales, etc., do not (at least until now) belong to independent countries.

to do with Newton's laws than with the bad luck of a football player? How many of us are aware that if we know the magnitude and direction of the force exerted on the ball, we can use mathematical equations to determine the exact position at which it will end up?

Newton's Laws

Newton's famous three laws of motion are stated as follows:

- A body that is at rest or is moving with a constant velocity will remain in this state as long as no external force is acted upon it.

- For a body with a constant mass, the total force acting on it is equal to its mass (m) times the acceleration (a) that it obtains, i.e.,

$$F = ma$$

- If a body exerts a force (action) on another body then the second body will also exert a force (reaction) of equal magnitude and opposite direction on the first one.

By using football as our case study, we can present all three of the above laws. When a ball is set for a free kick, it will remain stationary until a force is applied from the foot of a player (1st law). When the foot exerts the force, the ball will also apply an equal and opposite force on the foot (3rd law).

Finally, the 2nd law exhibits itself as follows: Once the ball leaves the foot, two forces are exerted on it during its flight; its weight (vertically downwards) and the air resistance (opposing its motion). If there is also spin applied, then a third force appears, the so called *Magnus force*. This has a direction dependant on the direction of the spin (clockwise or anticlockwise) and is perpendicular to the axis of rotation of the ball. We will discuss the air resistance and Magnus force in more detail in later chapters. The point is though, that according to the 3rd law, the total effect of all three forces will be to provide the ball with an acceleration, in this way also determining its velocity and total trajectory.

The weight force often gets confused with the concept of mass, so it is worth at this point to clear up the issue. Mass is measured in kg whereas weight which is a force, is measured in Newtons. Mass is the measure of resistance of a body to any change in its state of motion and as we have previously mentioned, is a scalar quantity. It is much more difficult to move a body with a large mass than one with a small one. Also, the mass of a body does not change no matter where the body is positioned. Weight on the other hand is the force that is exerted by Earth on the body. Since it is a force, it is a vector quantity with a direction towards the center of the Earth. The formula that gives it is the well known,

$$W = mg$$

Where g, is the acceleration of gravity.

The acceleration of gravity g that a body acquires due to the gravitational pull is independent of the mass of the body but does depend on the geographical position. So for example, at the Equator it has a value of approximately 9.78m/s², whereas at the poles it is about 9.83m/s². This means that at the poles the body will weigh around 0.5% more than at the Equator. A typical football has a mass of 0.43kg. At the poles its weight will be 0.43*9.83 = 4.227N whereas at the Equator, 0.43*9.78 = 4.205N. Its weight has decreased but its mass of course has remained the same. If you wish to lose weight you should move to somewhere with a more tropical climate. Unfortunately this will not affect your mass which will not have changed at all.

Returning to the trajectory of the ball, what is important for our analysis is that since it is under the influence of several forces, according to

An Introduction To The Physics Of Sports

the 2nd law, the ball will acquire an acceleration. Due to this acceleration the velocity and the position of the ball will change. The relative magnitude and direction of the three forces (W, weight, D, air resistance, F_M, Magnus force), will determine the exact form of the trajectory. Since the forces are vector quantities, they can also be represented by arrows in the same way that we showed for velocity in the previous chapter.

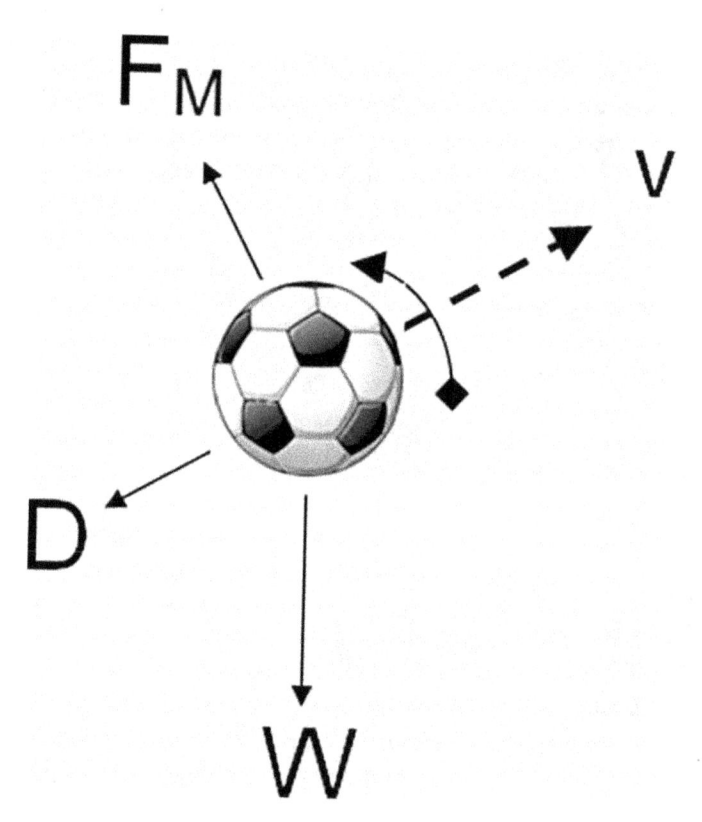

Figure 2.1: Forces acting on a football

In order to calculate the acceleration, velocity and position of the ball at each instant, we must solve a series of complex equations based on Newton's three laws. This is where the shooting ability of each footballer comes into play. The player substitutes the calculations required to solve complex equations with his experience and talent.

Chapter 2: Newton on the ball

As it can be seen in the following diagram, the direction for example of the Magnus force (determined by the footballer's kick), will affect the trajectory of the ball. By giving the axis of rotation the appropriate inclination, the ball can move to the right, upwards or a combination of both. Newton and the footballer are in full cooperation.

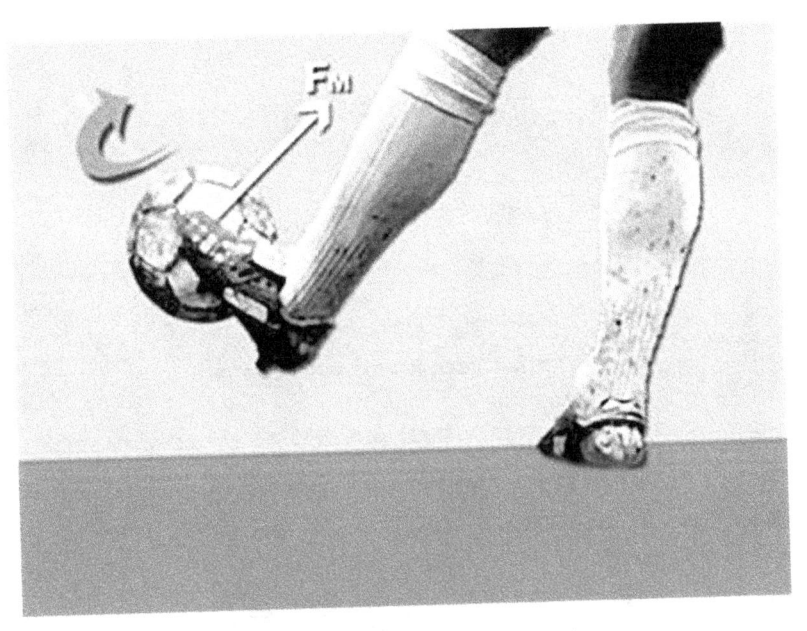

Figure 2.2: Magnus force and ball trajectory

A simple example

In order to get an idea of the trajectory the ball can take after a kick, we can look at a simple arithmetic example by making some simplifying assumptions. With Newton's help, we can determine the deflection of a ball due to spin for a free kick from 25m, with an initial ball speed of 30m/s and a spin rate of 7Hz. We will discuss more about rotational motion in the next chapter, just bear in mind for now that a rate of 7Hz implies that the ball completes seven revolutions round itself in each second.

An Introduction To The Physics Of Sports

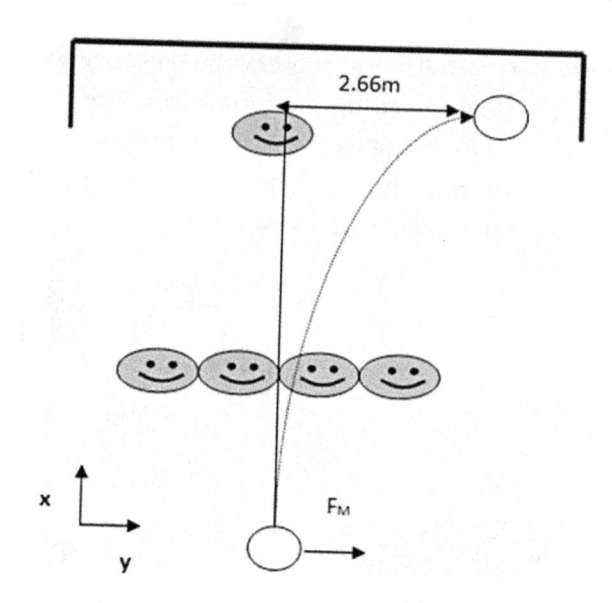

Figure 2.3: Free kick simple example

The assumptions we make are that the motion is confined to two dimensions (let us call them x and y), thus ignoring the height of the ball, and that the air resistance is zero. The air resistance is certainly not negligible but for the scope of our example the error produced by this assumption has only a negligible effect on the result.

Before we start, we must provide a formula for the Magnus force. For a football we can approximate its value with,

$$F_M = \pi^2 \rho R^3 V f$$

Where,
ρ is the air density
R is the radius of the ball
V is the ball speed
f is the ball spin rate[5]

---

[5] Where R3 = R*R*R

Chapter 2: Newton on the ball

The number π (pi), you may already know, is one of the most important mathematical constants and its value is approximately 3.14. The air density ρ, i.e. its mass per unit of volume, at a low altitude is roughly 1.2kg/m³.

So we have,

$$F_M = \pi^2 \rho R^3 V f = 3.14^2 \cdot 1.2 \cdot 0.11^3 \cdot 30 \cdot 7 = 3.3 N$$

According to Newton's 2nd law, this lateral force will produce a lateral acceleration,

$$a_y = \frac{3.3}{0.43} = 7.67 \frac{m}{s^2}$$

The time the ball takes to reach the goals can be found by dividing the distance x from where the free kick is taken to the ball speed[6]. Since the acceleration is assumed constant, according to the formula provided in the previous chapter we have,

$$y = \frac{1}{2}a_y t^2 = \frac{1}{2}a_y \left(\frac{x}{V}\right)^2 = \frac{1}{2} \times 7.67 \times \left(\frac{25}{30}\right)^2 = 2.66m$$

So even though significant simplifications have been assumed, our analysis shows that the ball will deflect by 2.66m and will end up in the right hand corner of the goal. The cooperation between player and Newton has been successful.

---

[6] From the formula of speed, $V = \frac{x}{t}$

A more detailed analysis

If we wish to perform a more detailed and precise analysis, we must fully solve the complex equations derived from the application of Newton's laws. Using suitable software, we can simulate the motion of a football for important aspects of the game, such as free kicks outside the penalty box and corner kicks. The technique that is evoked is similar to that employed by flight simulators and in simple terms can be described as follows. At each time instant we calculate the forces acting on the ball. From the forces, and by use of the 2nd law, we can estimate the acceleration. By knowing the acceleration at time t, we can estimate what the speed and the position will be after time δt, as long as δt is small enough (certainly smaller than 1 second). So basically, by determining the position and velocity of the ball at any given instant, we can calculate its new position and velocity at a time point a little later. By progressing in this way we can determine the whole trajectory.

We begin our simulation[7] with a free kick just outside the penalty box, 20 yards (18.28m) from the goal line. If the initial speed of the ball is 25m/s, the spin rate is 7Hz and the initial inclination of the ball trajectory is 17 degrees, we see from figure 2.4 that the ball ends up in the top left corner of the goal.

---

[7] This specific simulation was performed with the Matlab® software and the full analysis has been published in my paper, Spathopoulos, V. M, "Simulating Key Aspects of the Game of Soccer by Use of a Mathematical Model" (2009), e-journal of Science & Technology (e-JST), 4, 4, p. 57-65.

Chapter 2: Newton on the ball

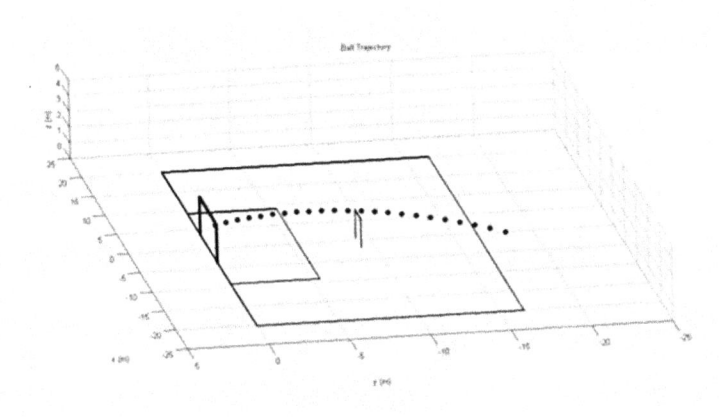

Figure 2.4: Free kick with 17 degrees inclination

For the next kick, we just increase the inclination by one degree, to 18 degrees. If we do this, the ball hits the bar.

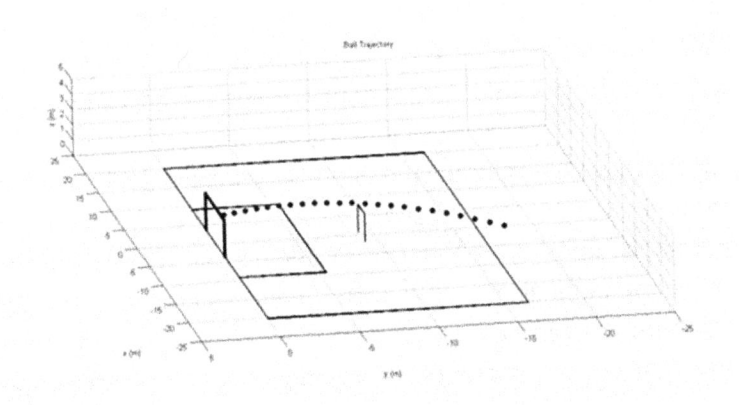

Figure 2.5: Free kick with 18 degrees inclination

Finally, if we reduce the inclination to 16 degrees, the ball hits the defenders' wall (positioned at a distance of 9.15m as determined by the rules).

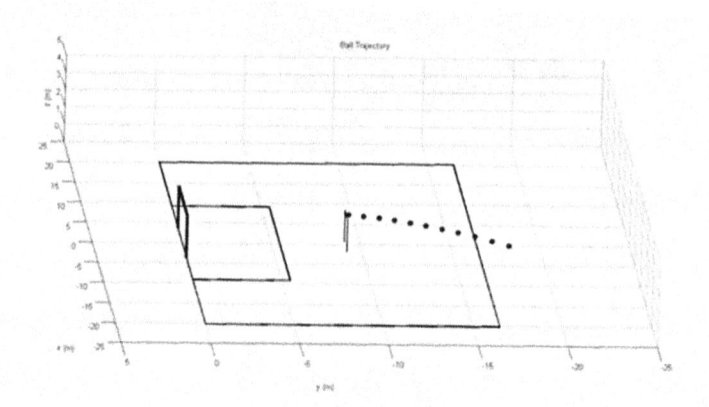

Figure 2.6: Free kick with 16 degrees inclination

It is very interesting that only a slight difference in the initial inclination given by the player modifies the final result by so much. Free kicks must be taken with an accuracy of 1 degree! In fact, by use of appropriate mathematical calculations, it can be shown that for the free kick simulated here, an error of 1 degree will produce a difference of 32cm to the height the ball will have when it crosses the goal line.

One of the most spectacular (and rare) occasions of goal scoring is by a direct corner kick. With our mathematical simulation, instead of defining the initial conditions of the kick (for example initial velocity, spin, etc), we can define the point at which we wish the ball to end up at and then get the computer to calculate the required initial conditions. So by setting the top right corner as our aim, our model finds the velocity, spin, etc., required. Of course there are an infinite number of combinations for which the outcome will be the same. In any case, the result (even at the level of a mathematical simulation) is truly impressive!

Chapter 2: Newton on the ball

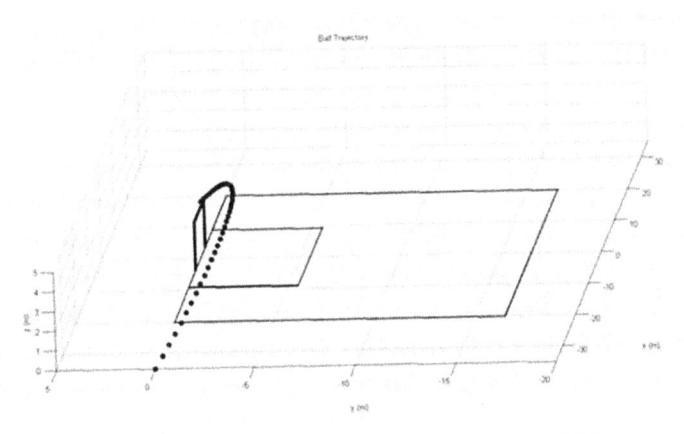

Figure 2.7: Goal scored from direct corner kick

Momentum

The *momentum* of a body is defined as the product of its mass times its speed. So for example, although the maximum speed of the shot in the shot put event is about half that of a football, its mass is sixteen times larger. The outcome is that the momentum of a shot is eight times that of a football. Momentum is a vector quantity and its direction is that of the velocity of the body.

Whenever a force is applied to a mass its momentum changes. Newton's 2nd law, in its more general form, can be expressed in relation to the change in momentum as follows: The force acting on a body is equal to the rate of change of its momentum.

The corresponding mathematical formula is,

$$F = \frac{\delta J}{\delta t}$$

Where δJ the change in momentum and δt is the time interval over which the force is applied.

For bodies with constant mass, this relationship is equivalent to our familiar *F=ma*, as the rate of change of momentum is equal to mass times the rate of change of speed, i.e. acceleration. The general form of the 2nd law is often more useful than the one containing the acceleration. If for example we drop a basketball, we can quite easily calculate the average force acting on it while it hits the ground.

Fontanella[8], has performed such experiments and measured the speed of a basketball before and after impact with the ground as 4.5m/s and 3.5m/s. A men's basketball has a mass of 0.61kg, so its momentum before and after impact is 4.5*0.61 = 2.745Ns and 3.5*0.61 = 2.131Ns, respectively. Since the velocities have opposite directions, we can easily find the total change in momentum by adding the two[9], as **4.88Ns**.

Fontanella also measured the time of contact of the ball and the ground as 0.016s. So the average force acting on the ball, according to the general form of the 2nd law, is **4.88/0.016 = 305N**. By ignoring the weight of the ball (which is much smaller), we see that the ground exerts a force on the ball that is approximately 300N. This is the average force; Fontanella also measured the maximum force as 650N. So a basketball also exerts (as a consequence of the 3rd law), a force on the ground that is roughly 100 times its weight, about the weight of an athlete. This is possibly the reason, that when playing this game (at a younger age), my fingers were constantly in pain.

Newton's 2nd law also tells us that for the same change in momentum, the acting force is smaller when the time interval over which it acts is greater (dividing by a larger number will produce a smaller result). This is exploited by athletes performing high jumps, for example a basketball player performing a "slam dunk". By bending his/her legs when

---

[8] See his book, Fontanella J.J., "The Physics of Basketball" (2006), John Hopkins University Press

[9] We do this whenever we need to subtract vector quantities with opposite directions.

landing, he/she will increase the time of contact with the ground, so decreasing the maximum force exerted on the legs. If the legs were kept straight, the team medics would have a lot of work to do.

Another consequence of the 2nd law is that if a body or system (group) of bodies does not have any external force acting on it (or the sum of forces is zero), then the total momentum remains unchanged. This principle is known as the *Principle of Conservation of Momentum*. To obtain an understanding, let us look at the sport of shooting. Before an athlete shoots with his/her rifle, the fact that the rifle is stationary means that its momentum is zero. As soon as a shot is taken, the bullet starts travelling in the forward direction and acquires a momentum in the same direction. In order for the total momentum to remain zero, a momentum must be created that is in the opposite direction. This is exactly the reason that we get the familiar rifle recoil.

We can use the Principle of Conservation of Momentum to estimate the consequences of a collision in sports. Let us for example, look at ice hockey, a particularly fast sport where the speeds reached by players can be as high as 40km/hr. Let us assume that one of them has a mass of 80kg and is moving towards the left with a speed of 9m/s and another with a mass of 90kg is moving in the opposite direction with a speed of 8m/s. Let us also assume that the athletes collide an essentially become a unified mass (something not particularly comfortable for them). What will their common speed be after the collision?

The athlete that is moving to the left will have a momentum of 80*9 = 720Ns. The opponent moving to the right will have 90*8 = 720Ns, i.e. the two momentums are equal. As we have already mentioned, since momentum is a vector quantity, and the athletes are moving in opposite directions, in order to find the total momentum before the collision we must subtract the two, which gives us a result of zero. As no external forces are acting on the players[10], the total momentum after

---

[10] Friction, which we will talk about in later chapters, is considered negligible.

the collision will remain zero. The only way for this to happen is for the two athletes locked together to remain stationary.

Coefficient of restitution

A basketball bounces more than a golf ball, the reason being that when colliding with the ground it suffers fewer energy losses. We will talk more about the concept of energy in a later chapter. At this point, we will determine the percentage of speed that the ball retains after the collision by use of the *coefficient of restitution*,

$$e = \frac{V_{after}}{V_{before}}$$

Where, V_{after} and V_{before} are the speeds before and after the collision.

The larger this parameter is, the more *elastic* the collision, i.e. the fewer the energy losses. Furthermore, if we let a ball drop from a certain height, the height that it will reach after the rebound is higher for balls with a greater coefficient of restitution. More specifically, it can be proved that the coefficient of restitution is approximately given by,

$$e = \sqrt{\frac{h_{after}}{h_{before}}}$$

Where, h_{after} and h_{before} are the heights after and before the collision.

The symbol $\sqrt{}$ is that of the *square root*, which is the number that when multiplied by itself will give the original number. So for example, the square root of 9 is 3.

For some sports, the heights at which the balls must rebound to are strictly defined. So in basketball, according to the International Basketball Federation (FIBA), if a ball is dropped from 1.8m it must return to a height between 1.2m and 1.4m. From the above formula we can deduce that the coefficient of restitution will lie between,

$$e = \sqrt{\frac{1.2}{1.8}} = 0.82 \text{ και } e = \sqrt{\frac{1.4}{1.8}} = 0.88$$

In the same way, if a tennis ball is dropped from a height of 100 inches (254cm) on to a concrete floor, it must rebound to a height between 53 inches (134.62cm) and 58 inches (147.32cm). So the limits are,

$$e = \sqrt{\frac{53}{100}} = 0.73 \text{ και } e = \sqrt{\frac{58}{100}} = 0.76$$

A basketball certainly bounces better than a tennis ball.

It is important to note that the coefficient e, depends not only on the type of ball but also on the properties of the ground. This is why the above limits are defined with respect to a concrete floor, as the tennis ball will certainly bounce differently on clay and on grass.

Another parameter that affects the value of the coefficient is temperature. If you are a golf player, it may be interesting to know that the coefficient of restitution of the golf ball drops from about 0.80 to 0.67 when it is cooled. It would make sense then, on a very cold day to keep the ball in your pocket, in order to maintain it at a higher temperature. This may also be the reason that short distance runners are supposed to perform better on warm days. At a higher temperature, the coefficient of restitution between shoe and ground will increase, thus helping the athletes.

Measuring the coefficient of restitution can constitute a simple physics experiment that you can plan yourselves. By dropping different types of balls you are able to perform calculations similar to the above. You can also realise the following simple study. In tennis rackets there exists a certain point from which, when the ball hits it, it rebounds with the highest speed. This point is called the *power point* or many times the "sweet point" [11] due to the nice sensation the athlete gets. By fixing a racket's arm to a table and letting its head be on the side you can drop a tennis ball from a suitable height (for example 0.5m) and then note how high it will rebound. You then repeat the process by letting the ball drop onto different points on the racket head. The point with the best rebound is the power point.

$$\text{momentum} = \frac{mv}{t}$$

$$J = mv$$

$$b = \frac{F}{t} \Rightarrow \frac{\Delta p}{\Delta t} \Leftarrow \frac{\text{change in momentum}}{\text{time interval}}$$

---

[11] The exact definition of the "sweet point" is actually more complicated.

Chapter 3: Rotational motion and impressive pirouettes

In the previous chapter we mentioned that the spin of a ball induces a force (the Magnus force) that affects its trajectory. We incur rotational motion both in our everyday life and in the world of sport. When we turn a bend with our car we know that this must be done carefully otherwise there is a danger of an accident. We are also aware of the fact that the road must have the right inclination (inwards) and that our speed must be within certain limits. Many of us have also admired the ability of cats to turn their bodies always managing to land on their legs with safety. This may be why it is rumored that they have nine lives.

We encounter rotational motion in many different sports. Such examples are throwing events like the discus and the hammer throwing, where the athlete must make a few turns before releasing the discus or the hammer. Even in some more "delicate" sports though, such as gymnastics, figure skating and diving, the number and quality of the pirouettes performed by the athlete to a great extent determines his/her overall performance.

The discus throw and angular speed

Before we correlate the angular speed with the performance of a discus thrower, we must first define it. In the first chapter we saw that speed is the rate of change of distance. We determine it by dividing the distance with the time taken to cover it. If the time interval is close (tends) to zero, we obtain the instantaneous speed, otherwise we have the average speed of the object.

Using the same logic, when a body is performing rotational motion, the *angular speed* is found if we divide the angle covered by the time taken to cover it. In this way, a discus thrower turning around himself with his arm extended provides the discus with an angular speed. If for example (see figure 3.1), the time taken for the discus to go from A to B is 0.04s, and the corresponding angle is 45 degrees, then the angular speed (or more correctly the average angular speed if this is not constant), will be 45/0.04 = 1125deg/s.

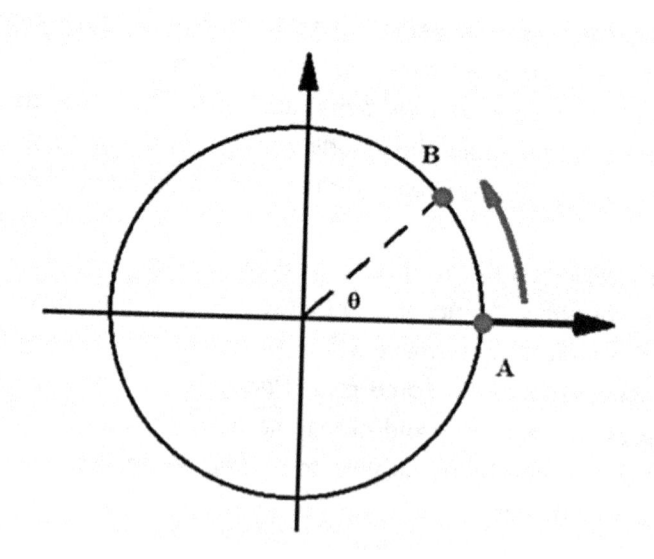

Figure 3.1: Angular speed of discus

A full circle has 360 degrees. When a discus thrower is turning with 1125deg/s he is completing 1125/360 = 3.125 revolutions per second. The units usually used by physicists are rad/s. One rad (radian) is a unit of angle, more specifically the angle that is formed if the radius of the circle covers an arc of length one radius, as seen in figure 3.2

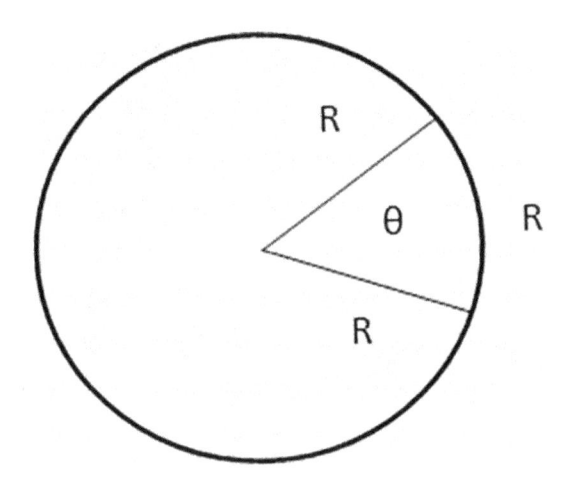

Figure 3.2: Definition of the radian

It can be proved that a full circle has 2*π rad, so it is easily deduced that 1 rad is approximately 57.3 deg. So in our case the angular speed of 1125deg/s is about 19.63rad/s.

It is evident that apart from the angle covered by a body performing circular motion, there is also a distance covered measured in meters. So for each circle of radius R that is completed, a distance of 2πR meters (the length of a circle as proven by the ancient Greeks) is also covered. This is performed over a certain time, so apart from the angular speed we also have a *linear* one (as it is termed in other to differentiate the two). We can prove that they are connected by,

$V = \Omega R$
Where Ω is the angular speed,
R is the radius of the circle covered by the body.

35

Let us suppose that our athlete is not very tall with an arm length of 0.6m. Then, with an angular speed of 19.63rad/s, the linear speed will be 19.63*0.6 = 11.78m/s. If on the other hand we are dealing with a tall athlete with long arms, for example 0.85m, the linear speed will be 19.63*0.85 = 16.69m/s. In this way the discus will acquire a higher linear speed and will therefore also be thrown at a greater range. It seems as though tall athletes have an advantage in this event due to the relationship between angular and linear speed. Relevant studies confirm this. It should be noted that in reality the arm of the discus thrower acts more like a whip rather than a rigid bar. With this technique, competitors can give the discus greater speeds that can reach 25m/s (90km/hr).

Centripetal force and gymnastics

We have seen that according to Newton, in order for the velocity of a body to change, a force must be exerted on it. This applies both to the magnitude of the velocity and its direction. When a body performs circular motion its direction is constantly changing and so is the direction of its linear velocity that is always perpendicular to the radius of the circle. This is the reason that that discus always starts its flight at a direction perpendicular to the arm of the athlete.

The force responsible for the change in the direction of a body in turning motion is called the *centripetal force* and always has a direction towards the center of the circular path. The centripetal force is not an independent force in the way as forces such as weight, air resistance, etc., may be considered. In order for circular motion to be possible, some resultant force must be acting on the body with a direction always to the center of the circle. This resultant force will play the role of the centripetal force, whose magnitude is given by,

$$F_c = m\Omega^2 R$$

Chapter 3: Rotational motion and impressive pirouettes

Where m is the body mass,
Ω is the angular speed
R is the radius of the circle.

In the case of discus throwing, the force that acts as the centripetal force is that exerted by the hand of the thrower onto the discus. The hand is constantly turning (until the throw) so the force it exerts on the discus fulfils the aforementioned direction requirements. A similar situation occurs when a cyclist racing in a velodrome (arena for track cycling) takes a tight turn. Velodromes have track inclinations that may be higher than 45deg. This design helps to provide the forces acting on the athlete with the necessary direction to become centripetal.

Another interesting application of the above is found in gymnastics and in particular in the high bar event, one of six events in men's gymnastics[12]. One of the basic routines performed is that of the giant circle, in which several complete revolutions are executed as depicted in the following figure.

It is interesting to study what happens in positions A and B where the analysis is simpler due to the fact that the weight acts in the direction of the radius of the circle covered by the athlete. With simple calculations based on energy transformations (more about this in the next chapter), we can estimate that the angular speed in position B for an athlete of mass m = 60kg, assuming that his mass[13] performs a circle of radius R = 1m and that he starts from position A with zero angular speed, will be about 5.8rad/s. Although this value is a little higher than those actually achieved, it is still quite a good approximation. If we estimate the centripetal force required to sustain such a value, we have,

$$F_c = m\Omega^2 R = 60 \cdot 5.8^2 \cdot 1 = 2018.4N$$

---

[12] The numerical data for this application are taken from the publication, Hiley M.J., Yeadon M.R., "Swinging around the high bar" (2001), Physics Education, 14-17.
[13] More precisely, the center of gravity of the athlete, as discussed in the next chapter.

An Introduction To The Physics Of Sports

Figure 3.3: Giant circle

At the lowest point of the circle the two forces acting on the athlete are his weight and the force from the bar. More specifically, the force from the bar acts towards the center of the circle whereas the weight is in the opposite direction, towards the ground. We know that when two vector quantities, such as forces, act in opposite directions, in order to find the resultant (total) force, we must subtract one from the other. In this case, the resultant force is the centripetal force so we have,

Chapter 3: Rotational motion and impressive pirouettes

$$F_c = F_{bar} - W = 2018.4N$$

Where F_{bar} is the force exerted from the bar.

To estimate this force and so (according to Newton's 3rd law) the force exerted from the athlete onto the bar, we must add the weight to the centripetal force. We know that the weight is given by W=mg and so is about ten times the mass of the athlete. We thus obtain,

$$F_{bar} = F_c + W = 2018.4 + 600 = 2618.4N$$

So we see that our simple model shows us that at the lowest point of his trajectory the athlete exerts a force on the bar which is more than four times his weight. In reality this force will be slightly smaller. In any case though, this performance (although strictly speaking of course, not comparable) surpasses that of weight lifters!

All of the above can be viewed more clearly by use of a simulation. The model is very simple but gives us a good impression of what is actually happening. The results are provided in the following figures.

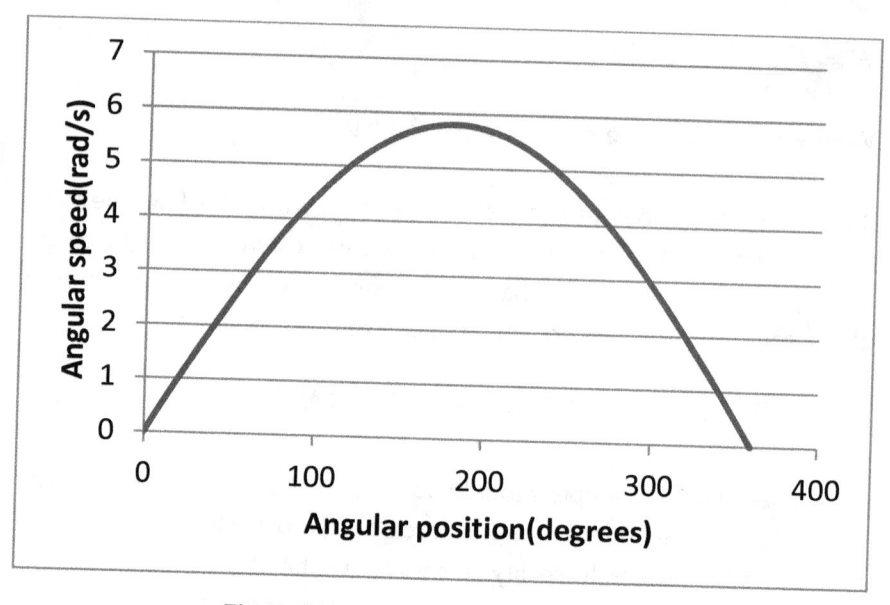

Figure 3.4: Variation of angular speed

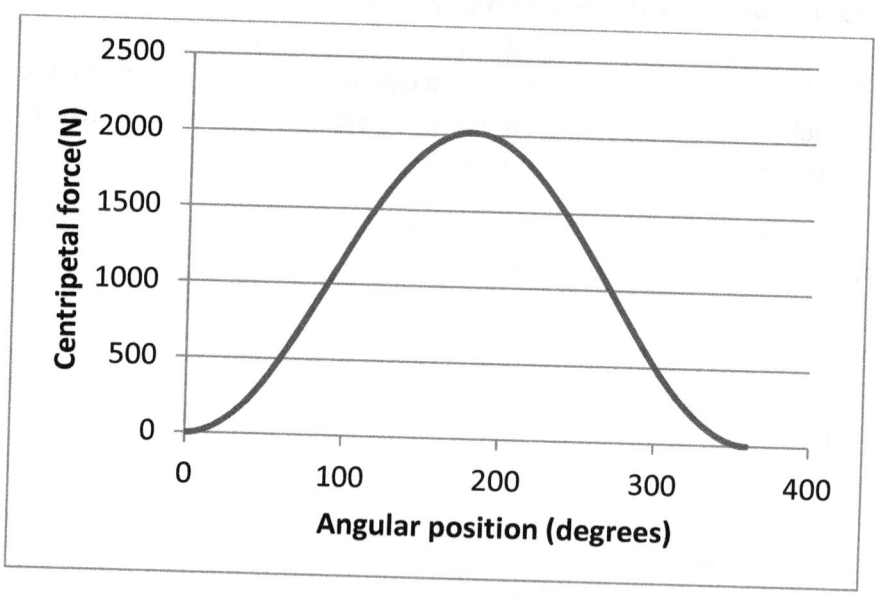

Figure 3.5: Variation of centripetal force

Chapter 3: Rotational motion and impressive pirouettes

From the above we can observe the way in which the angular speed and centripetal force vary in accordance to the angular position of the athlete, who starts at the highest point (angular position zero degrees) and completes a full circle. As expected, the maximum angular speed and so the maximum centripetal force is obtained at 180 degrees, i.e. at the lowest point of the trajectory.

Contestants in this event often perform accelerating circles, which result in a non-zero angular speed at the top of the circle. At this point, the weight and the force from the bar act in the same direction (downwards), so the vectors are added to each other:

$$F_c = F_{bar} + W$$

To find the force F_{bar}, we have,

$$F_{bar} = W - F_c$$

We see that if F_c becomes equal to the weight, the athlete does not feel any forces; in effect he is in weightless flight. It is interesting to establish at what angular speed this occurs at. We have:

$$F_c = W = 600N$$

So:

$$m\Omega^2 R = 600$$

By use of simple algebra we can deduce that this will happen at an angular speed a little larger than 3rad/s, so the athlete is completing about half a circle per second.

Angular momentum and pirouettes

We know that the resistance of a body to a change in its linear velocity is represented by its mass. When dealing with rotational motion the equivalent quantity determining the resistance to turning motion, is the *moment of inertia* of the body.

The moment of inertia, although related to mass, does not depend only on its value but also on its distribution about the axis of rotation. It increases as the distribution moves further away from the axis. This is the reason that bodies of similar mass but of different shape will turn in a different way. As we will see, the athletes in sports such as figure skating and diving use this to their advantage.

Just as the moment of inertia is the quantity equivalent to mass, *angular momentum* is the equivalent of momentum (more correctly, linear momentum) and its magnitude is given by:

$H = I\Omega$

Where, I is the moment of inertia about the axis of rotation.

Angular momentum is the result of applying torque to a body. *Torque* (or *moment*), is the quantity equivalent to force for turning motion. It is defined as the product of the acting force times its distance from the axis of rotation (see figure 3.6). For greater distances we have a greater magnitude of torque. We realise this when pushing a seesaw. If we wish to push our side down then we need less force when we push at a distance from the axis of rotation than if this is done closer to the axis.

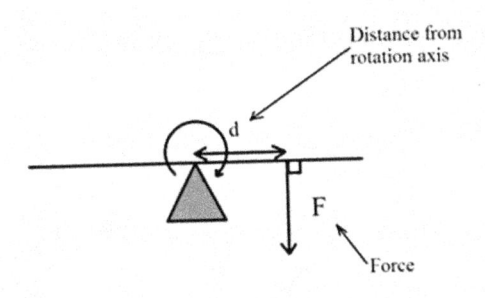

Figure 3.6: Application of torque

Pirouettes on ice and in the air

When no external torques are applied on a body (or more correctly the resultant torque is zero), then the angular momentum of the body remains constant. This is the *Principle of Conservation of Angular Momentum*, essentially the application of Newton's 1st law to rotational motion. One of the most impressive applications of this is encountered in figure skating and in particular during the pirouettes executed by the contestants. At the start of the pirouette the athlete increases her moment of inertia by extending her hands and leg and so distributing more mass further away from the axis of rotation.

In this way she attains a large angular momentum without having to increase her angular speed. She then pulls her hands and leg in and so decreases her moment of inertia. As the angular momentum remains constant (there is no external torque present), the angular speed must increase. Just like magic, the athlete starts to turn faster with an angular speed ω_2 much greater than ω_1. The angular speeds in this sport can reach values of over 40rad/s, i.e. almost 7 revolutions per second or 420 revolutions per minute. This is approximately the same as the engine of a car in neutral.

An Introduction To The Physics Of Sports

Figure 3.7: Angular momentum and figure skating

A similar mechanism manifests itself in diving. An athlete performing a summersault is depicted in figure 3.8. At the beginning with her body extended, she has quite a large moment of inertia. She then curls up (in position A) and as a result her moment of inertia is reduced and her angular speed is increased. At the end of the dive, the procedure is reversed with the moment of inertia increasing (at position B) in order for the entry into the water to occur with the smallest possible rotational movement. During the whole dive the angular momentum remains constant.

Chapter 3: Rotational motion and impressive pirouettes

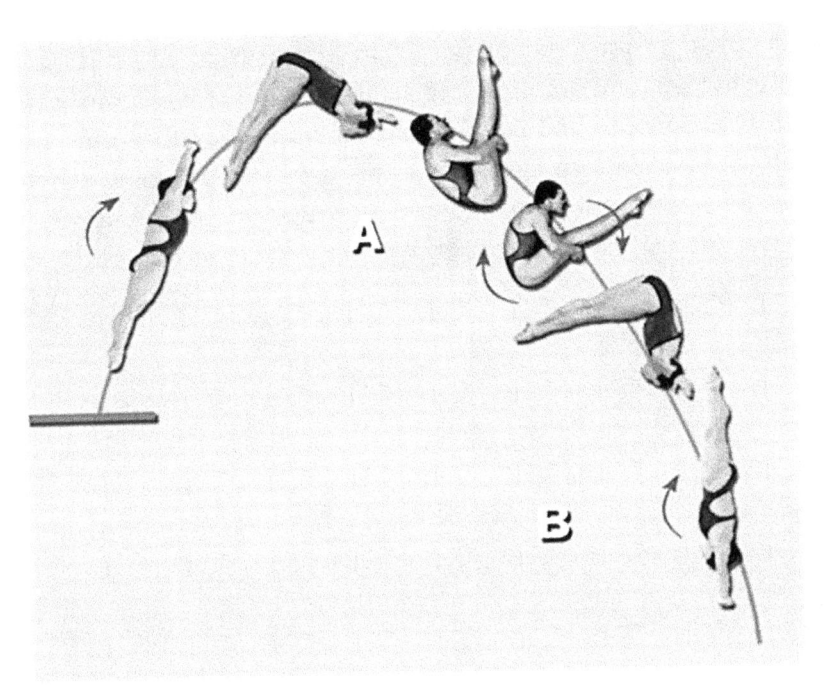

Figure 3.8: Angular momentum and diving

The ideal landing system

The flexibility of cats would make them very good athletes. Their nine lives may also be due to the principle of angular momentum. Their ability to always land on their feet no matter how awkward their fall is, is surely admirable.

It seems weird that even if a cat starts its fall with zero angular speed (and so momentum), it can still land on its feet. How can it turn when its initial angular momentum is zero?

The full answer is quite complex from a physics point of view, though it is related directly to the flexibility of their body. By turning one part of their body in one direction (for example their front legs) and the other part in the opposite direction (for example their back legs), it is like two angular momentums are produced acting in opposite directions. Just like when two opposite and equal forces act on a body they cancel each other out having a zero net effect, so the total angular momentum (that is also a vector quantity), will remain zero. By performing the right maneuvers, cats are able to land safely without violating any physical laws.

Chapter 4: High energy sports

When we refer to sport, concepts such as fatigue, energy expense, and caloric consumption come immediately to mind. How do these concepts relate to the laws of physics and what are the physical quantities that determine the effectiveness of athletes? In this chapter, we will learn about the ways in which contestants manage, by transforming one form of energy to another, to achieve impressive results such as superhuman six meter jumps in the pole vault and speeds that even motored vehicles would be envious of, in cycling.

Center of gravity

Before we analyse the concepts of work and energy, it is necessary to discuss the *center of gravity* of a body. Every, body and thus the athletes themselves, is made up of individual components each of which has its own weight. So our weight is just the sum of individual weights, of components such as our arms, legs, etc. The point, about which the distribution of these individual weights is symmetrical, is the center of gravity of the body. Thus, if a body has more mass distributed in its upper part, the center of gravity will be closer to the top of the body. This applies to humans, as the center of gravity of an average person is located approximately at a height of 1 meter, thus being above the waist.

There are two properties of the center of gravity that have a great impact on sport. First of all its location is dependent on the shape of the body. So if the same body is to take a different shape, the position of the center of gravity will shift. An athlete that bends his/her legs will lower his/her center of gravity position. This, amongst other things, will result in greater stability, something especially important in sports such as wrestling. Also, and this may sound the strangest, the center of gravity can lie entirely outside the body itself. For example, if the body is hollow it will literally be positioned somewhere in the air. As we will discuss later on, during the Olympic Games in Mexico, in 1968, an, until then unknown athlete, the American Dick Fosbury, came from nowhere to teach the world about both of these properties.

Work in physics

In physics, the concept of *work* is defined in a very specific way, contrary to our everyday life where work can range from drawing a picture to watering our garden. When a force moves a body, it is said that the force produces *mechanical work*. If it is in the same direction as the displacement of the body, then the work produced is equal to the product of the force times the distance covered:

$W = FS$

Let us take for example the work produced from the force exerted by a weightlifter on the bar when a weight of 1500N (i.e. with a mass of roughly 150kg) is lifted by 2m. The athlete will have to apply a force that is at least equal to the weight and so the work produced is equal to 1500*2 = 3000J. The unit of work, Joule, is the work produced when a force of one Newton displaces a body by one meter.

From the above we deduce that when a body remains stationary, no work is produced. An athlete sitting while waiting for his/her turn to compete does not produce any work and thus will not tire (maybe only psychologically). The possibility exists though that even if a body is moved and a force is applied, the force does not produce any work. This occurs when the force acts in a direction that is perpendicular to the motion. So when an athlete is running on a horizontal road, the weight which acts perpendicular to the path does not produce any work.

It is also important to note that the work done by a force can be positive or negative. When the force is in the same direction as the displacement it actually offers energy to the body. When the force is in the opposite direction it opposes the motion, subtracting energy from the body and thus the work done is negative. This is easily anticipated by a cyclist. When he/she is going downhill, then gravity (or at least part of it) is in the direction of motion of the bike and will offer positive work making the ride easier. But whatever goes down must also go up and in this case gravity works against the rider by doing negative work. I feel the effect every time I go up the hill leading to my house.

Power and cycling

In physics in general and especially in the physics of sport, we are often more interested in the rate of change of a quantity than in the quantity itself. The same applies to work done; we are usually more interested in the rate in which it is produced, a measure of the effectiveness of an athlete.

By dividing work with the time interval over which it was produced, we find the value of *power*, which is measured in Watts. So in order to estimate power we have:

$$P = \frac{W}{t} = \frac{FS}{t} = F\frac{S}{t}$$

An Introduction To The Physics Of Sports

The quotient though of distance over time gives us speed, so power can also be derived from the product of force times speed, a relationship that can prove useful in many cases.

We can apply the above to study the performance of a cyclist. In order to do this I have used simple equations like those developed by Hannas and Goff[14] to predict the performance of athletes in the Tour de France of 2003. Although the model is relatively simple, it predicted the total time of the winner with great accuracy.

I will explain its logic for the simple case of a horizontal (without inclination) path. We assume that three horizontal forces are exerted; the forward thrust from the athlete (F_{cyc}), and the resistive ones, friction (F_{fr}) and the air resistance (D). The perpendicular forces (weight (W) and (F_{gr}) from the ground), as we know produce no work.

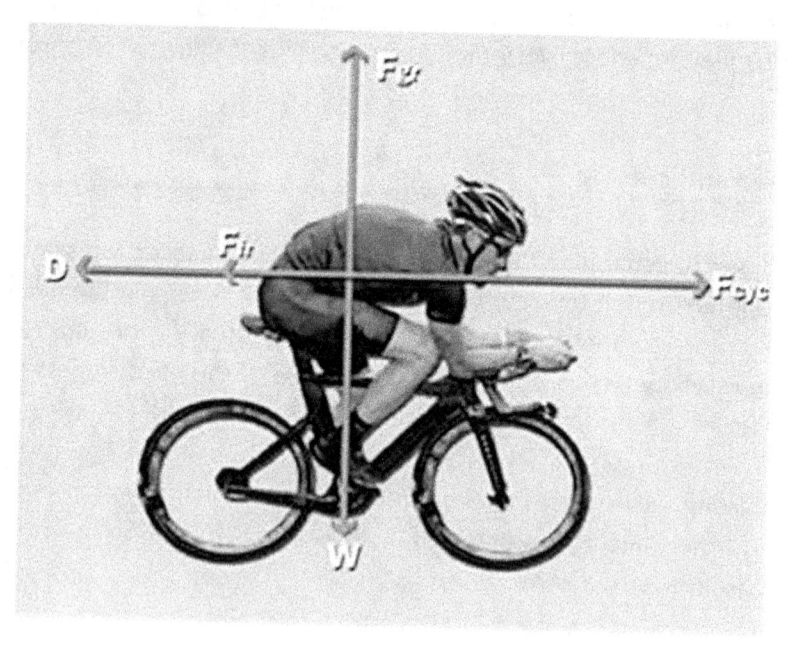

Figure 4.1: Forces acting on a cyclist

---

[14] See the publication, Hannas B.L. and Goff J.E., "Model of the 2003 Tour de France" (2004), American Journal of Physics, 72(5), 575-579.

Let us suppose that our athlete is able to achieve a constant power (375W is considered a suitable value), then the thrust force can be calculated as the quotient of power over speed (as we showed earlier that P=FV). I have mentioned that we will discuss air resistance in later chapters, but any of us that have cycled will have felt its effect.

As far as friction is concerned, this is the force that results from the relative motion of two bodies in contact and manifests itself due to the bonds that are formed between the molecules of the two bodies. It is the reason that we are able to walk, without it making a step would be a very slippery business (just try and walk on ice where the friction is minimal). In our example it appears due to the contact of the bicycle wheels with the ground. The relevant formula is:

$$F_{fr} = \mu F_{gr}$$

Where F_{gr} is the ground reaction,
μ is the coefficient of friction.

The coefficient of friction is a pure number (with no units) that characterises the resistance to the motion between two bodies due to friction. For the case of the bicycle and the ground we can assume a value of 0.003.

Taking the above into account, one can program the equations derived from the application of Newton's 2nd law (the force resultant is equal to the mass times the resulting acceleration). The interesting results are portrayed in the following figures.

14
12
10
8
6
4
2
0

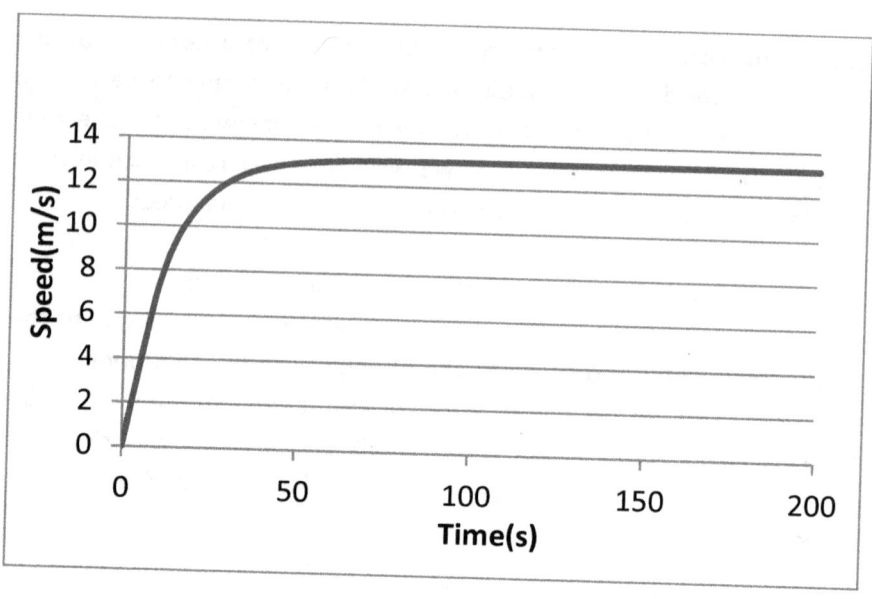

Speed(m/s)

0   50   100   150   200
           Time(s)

Figure 4.2: Variation of speed

In the first graph we have the variation of speed with time. The cyclist starts from rest and reaches a maximum speed of about 13m/s (47km/hr). The acceleration reduces to zero since on the one hand the thrust force becomes progressively smaller (as the power which is the product of thrust times speed remains constant), and on the other hand the air resistance increases (we will see in a later chapter that it is proportional to the square of speed).

Essentially, the athlete produces work through the action of his legs, contrary to the friction and air resistance that subtract energy from the system. Which of the two forces though (friction or air resistance) is responsible for the most losses? In other words, for which of the two does the cyclist spend more power to overcome? I have asked this question several times and the instinctive answer is usually that the friction between wheels and ground results in the most power losses.

The right answer though is provided in the following figure where the percentage of losses due to air resistance is presented in relation to the speed of the bicycle.

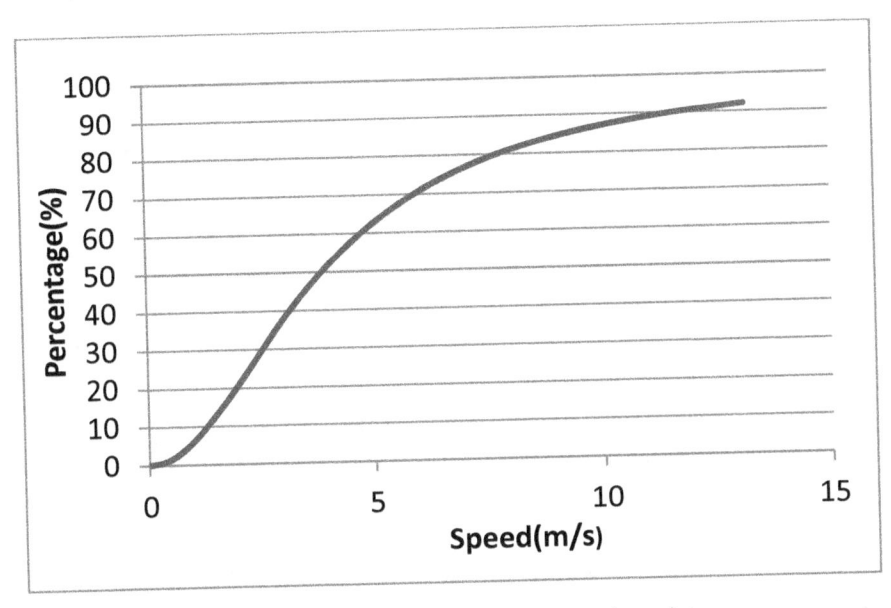

Figure 4.3: Percentage of losses due to air resistance

We can see that for speeds above 4m/s most losses are due to the air resistance. If we think that this is the speed for a brisk jog and that the average speed for a cyclist competing in the Tour de France is over 11m/s, we deduce that over 90% of the power is used to overcome air resistance. When you are cycling, make sure that the wind is on your side.

I mentioned previously that when taking the uphill road leading to my house I usually end up exhausted. The negative effect of weight can be revealed by our simulation. In figure 4.4 the variation of speed for an uphill road inclined at 0.1rad (about 5.7 degrees), is presented.

The power produced by the athlete will be larger, at 500W (from the 375 assumed for the straight path). Despite this increase in power production and thus in the resulting fatigue, the maximum speed achieved does not surpass 6m/s.

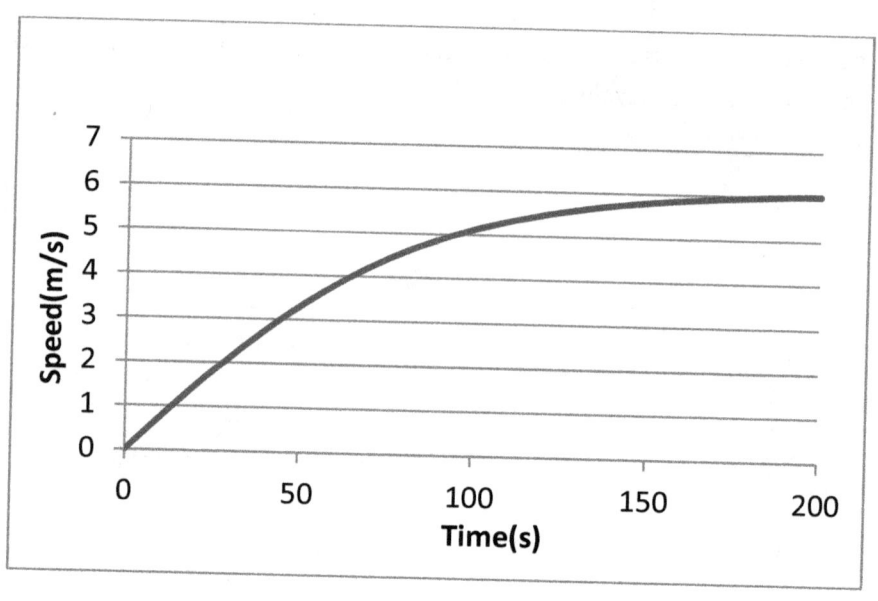

Figure 4.4: Variation of speed for an inclined path

There is not much athletes can do regarding the negative effect of weight when going up a hill. In order to reduce the effect of air resistance though, several methods have been deployed. Between 65-80% of the total deceleration is due to the presence of the athlete himself. If he/she takes a more crouched position, with the head down, then the magnitude of the resisting force can be reduced by about 25%. Special, aerodynamically designed helmets can also produce a reduction of 2%. Further improvement is achieved through the design of the bicycle itself. Finally, in a race with many participants, the ones that are not in the lead will incur a smaller air resistance due to the fact that they are in a sense "protected" by the leaders. This phenomenon is termed "drafting' and can result in an energy saving of about 30-40%. The athlete deciding to take the lead must have planned this well. This is why in team events, the team members will usually take turns in leading the race.

Chapter 4: High energy sports

Mechanical energy

The concept of energy in physics is not something that can easily be explained in simple terms. We often hear of its various forms such as solar, nuclear and thermal. Generally speaking we can say that energy is the ability of a body to produce work. From the point of view of sports, we are mainly interested in mechanical energy, i.e. the energy a body has due to its position in relation to Earth and to its speed (linear and angular). The first type of energy is known as *potential* energy and the second type as *kinetic* energy.

Potential energy is given by the formula:

$$E_{pot} = mgh$$

Where *h* is the height of the body from the surface of the Earth.

If we return to our original example with the weightlifter, when the weights are lifted, they are at a height of 2m and their potential energy is 1500*2 = 3000J (the same as the work done by the athlete). We do not know how high the apple that fell on Newton's head was, what we do know is that the higher it was the greater the potential energy and so the larger its effect on the head of the great scientist.

On the other hand, when the apple reaches the height of the head it has lost most of its potential energy, so how is the pain caused? What has happened is that it has now acquired kinetic energy due to its speed; this energy is given by the formula:

$$E_{kin} = \frac{1}{2}mV^2$$

So the kinetic energy greatly increases with increasing speed, it does depend though also on the mass of the body. In many sports the aim of

An Introduction To The Physics Of Sports

the contestants is to give to a body the highest possible speed, so it would be interesting to estimate the corresponding kinetic energies.

Sport	Mass (kg)	Maximum speed (m/s)	Kinetic energy (J)
Hammer throw (men)	7.257	25	2268
Shot put (men)	7.26	15	817
Discus (men)	2	24	576
Javelin (men)[15]	0.8	30	360
Football	0.43	30	194
Golf	0.046	75	129
Tennis	0.057	67	128
Table tennis	0.0027	35	1.65

Table 4.1: Kinetic energies in various sports

The undisputed winner is the hammer throw, with a kinetic energy of about 2270J. The combination of mass and speed is unique for this event. The amount of energy that must be transferred from the hammer throwers to the hammer is great and so is the strength required of the athletes.

Is it only the strength of the athletes that determine the kinetic energy achieved in a sport? Certainly not, if this were the case then it would be deduced from the table that a footballer is two times stronger than a tennis player. The determining factor is actually which muscles are involved in transferring the energy from the athlete to the body that acquires it. For a football kick the leg muscles are stronger than those of the arm and shoulder, i.e. the ones used primarily in tennis.

Until now we used the Joule and Watt in order to measure energy (work) and power. In actual fact there are other units that are probably

---

[15] In the corresponding women's events the values for the mass and speed are lower.

Chapter 4: High energy sports

more familiar to us, such as calories and horse power. Just imagine yourself asking in a supermarket how many Joules are contained in a yogurt, or a car salesman, how many Watts a car engine can produce. How do the units we are familiar with relate to the ones normally preferred by physicists?

Starting with the relationship between Joules and calories, 1Kcal is equal to 4184 Joules. We can thus estimate the kinetic energy of a hammer (in the men's event) as approximately 0.54Kcal. So a kebab will contain more than 1000 times the calories of a hammer in flight! If you think you eat too much this piece of information may help you go on a diet. On the other hand, 1HP (horsepower) is equal to 745.7 Watt, so the cyclist in our simulation on a straight path will produce a power of about 0.5HP. How much horsepower does an actual horse produce? According to relevant studies, a horse can produce a maximum of 14.9HP. This power output can only be achieved for a few seconds. For long hours of agricultural work, 1HP does seem a good estimate.

Returning to mechanical energy, there is a fundamental principle in physics that states that if there is no energy exchange between a body and its environment then the total mechanical energy, i.e. the sum of the potential and kinetic energies, will remain constant. In other words, when a body loses height it will gain speed and vice versa. The story with the apple hitting Newton's head verifies this.

The key here though, is that when we refer to potential energy, when we say that its value depends on the position of the body, what we actually mean is the position of the center of gravity of the body. Potential energy is related to the work done by gravity so it makes sense that it depends on the point on which this force acts on. Dick Fosbury may not have known this; he did anticipate very well though, the practical consequences.

The high jump, the pole vault and mechanical energy

When a high jump athlete takes off, he/she transforms part of his/her kinetic energy that is produced during the sprint, to potential energy. If the mechanical energy that can be produced is predetermined, is there any other way in which the chances of successfully clearing the bar can be improved? As we have already mentioned, in 1968, Dick Fosbury used a new technique that to his honor was named the "Fosbury Flop", to show how this could be done.

With the techniques used until then, both the athletes themselves and their center of gravity cleared the bar. For example with the "scissors" technique, one of the first deployed, the center of gravity would clear the bar by about 25-30cm (see figure 4.5)

Figure 4.5: The scissors technique

The revolution brought by Fosbury is portrayed in the following figure.

Chapter 4: High energy sports

Figure 4.6: The Fosbury Flop

The truly ingenious leap (!) in the technique was that by clearing the bar with his back and by changing the shape of his body in the way seen, the athlete could clear the bar without his center of gravity having to also clear it. By this change in body shape he was able to move his center of gravity outside his body. So without having to increase his mechanical energy, he was successful with his jump.

The principle of mechanical energy conservation is also utilized by pole vault athletes (see, figure 4.7). Let us use some simple calculations to see how. A good athlete during the run up can achieve a maximum speed of about 10m/s. Let us suppose that he has a mass of 70kg, so that his kinetic energy when he reaches the takeoff point is about 3500J. If we assume that his center of gravity is about 1m form the ground then he will also have a potential energy of 700J and his mechanical energy will be 4200J. By use of the pole, he transforms all of this mechanical energy to potential energy, so we have 4200 = 70*10*h, where h is the maximum height he achieves. From the last equation we can estimate h to be 6m, a good approximation for this event.

It should be noted that in reality there will be some energy losses when the pole is placed on the ground, just before his flight begins. These losses are countered by the athlete himself who uses his arms to push the pole while in the air in order to obtain extra thrust, thus producing more work.

Figure 4.7: Mechanical energy conservation principle and the pole vault

So why is it that athletes of the high jump cannot produce similar records? It is certain that they can achieve similar if not higher maximum speeds (as they are not carrying a pole), so their kinetic energy will be at least the same. The problem here is that high jumpers do not have to their disposal the very efficient means of transforming energy that a pole vault athlete has, i.e. the pole itself. Humans themselves are not very good in transforming kinetic energy to potential energy, so most of the energy during a high jump is lost, meaning that the current world record for men is only (!) 2.45m and for women, 2.09m.

Even in the pole vault event though the ability of the pole to transform kinetic to potential energy depends to a great extent on the materials used for its construction. Until the beginning of the 1960s, the poles used by athletes were made from bamboo. At that point technological advancement resulted in more sophisticated and flexible materials such as fiberglass, being used. The impact on the performance of the athletes can be studied through the progress of the world record in the men's event. If we take the period from 1941 until 1961, the record increased from 4.72m to 4.83m, so in 20 years there was an increase of only 11cm. From 1961 until 1981 the record improved to 5.81m, i.e. an increase of almost 1m. The progress after the introduction of new materials was almost ten times that of the period when bamboo was used.

An extreme sport

The variations in the potential and kinetic energy of an athlete can be observed through a sport that belongs to those often termed as extreme. Skydiving is the sport in which brave men and women jump out of an aircraft, usually from a height of a few kilometers, free falling until the deployment of their parachute. During their flight, a few interesting transformations of energy take place and these can be studied by use of a simple simulation. We assume that our athlete has a mass of 80kg and jumps from a height of 4200m. We also assume that the fall occurs without the presence of a horizontal velocity component (which will in reality exist due to the forward velocity of the aircraft).

An Introduction To The Physics Of Sports

Figure 4.8: Forces in skydiving

We will examine two different cases. For the first one we will suppose that the jump takes place in a vacuum, i.e. without the presence of the atmosphere. With this assumption, the air resistance becomes zero and the only force acting on the athlete is the weight force. This implies that there is no energy exchange between the athlete and the environment and so the principle of mechanical energy conservation will hold. In the following figure the variation of potential energy (dark line) and kinetic energy (lighter line) is presented for such a case. The variation is presented for a fall of 3000m, after which we hope that the parachute will open. As expected, the kinetic energy increases by the same amount as the potential energy decreases, since there are no energy losses in a vacuum.

Chapter 4: High energy sports

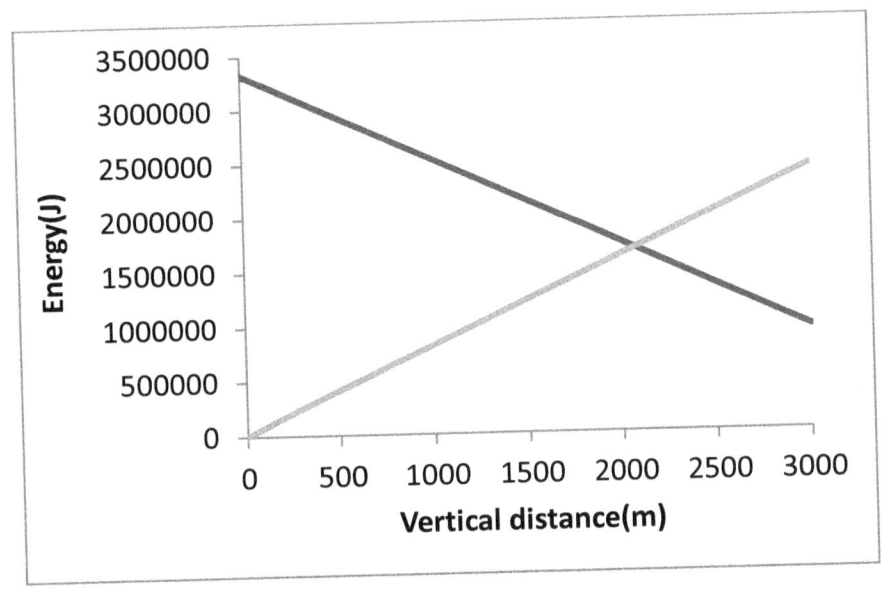

Figure 4.9: Variation of potential and kinetic energy in a vacuum

In reality of course, just like with the bicycle, the air resistance will subtract energy from the athlete. In figure 4.10 we see that although the potential energy decreases at the same rate as it did in the vacuum, the kinetic settles to a much smaller value. The difference is due to the presence of the atmosphere.

It is also interesting to observe how the speed of the athlete varies. In the following figure we see that a final speed is reached that in physics is called *terminal velocity*. When this speed is achieved, the two forces acting on the athlete (the weight and the air resistance) become equal and as they are in opposite directions, the total force will be zero. According to Newton's 1st law, the velocity will remain constant, as we can see at a value of 51m/s, i.e. the athlete is falling at 184km/hr.

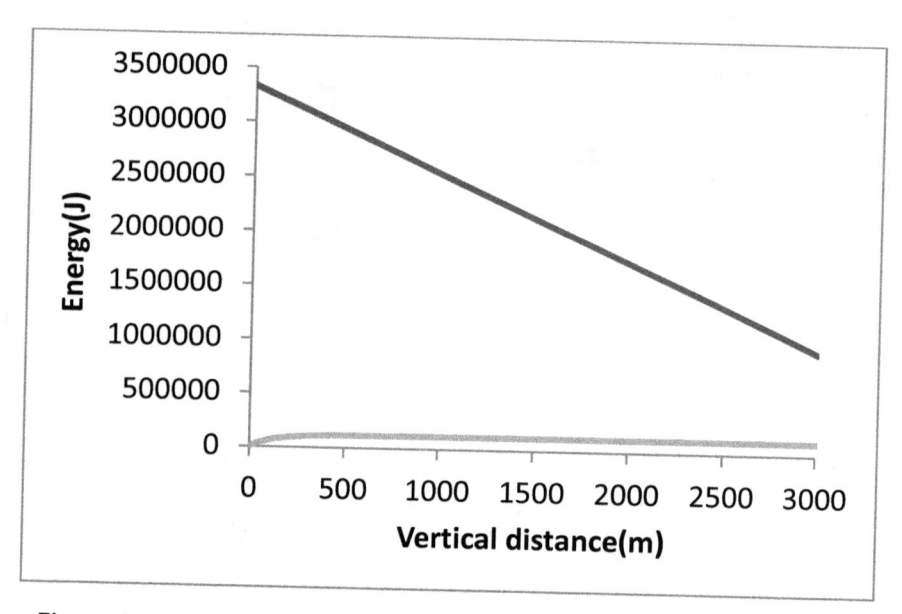

Figure 4.10: Variation of potential and kinetic energy in the atmosphere

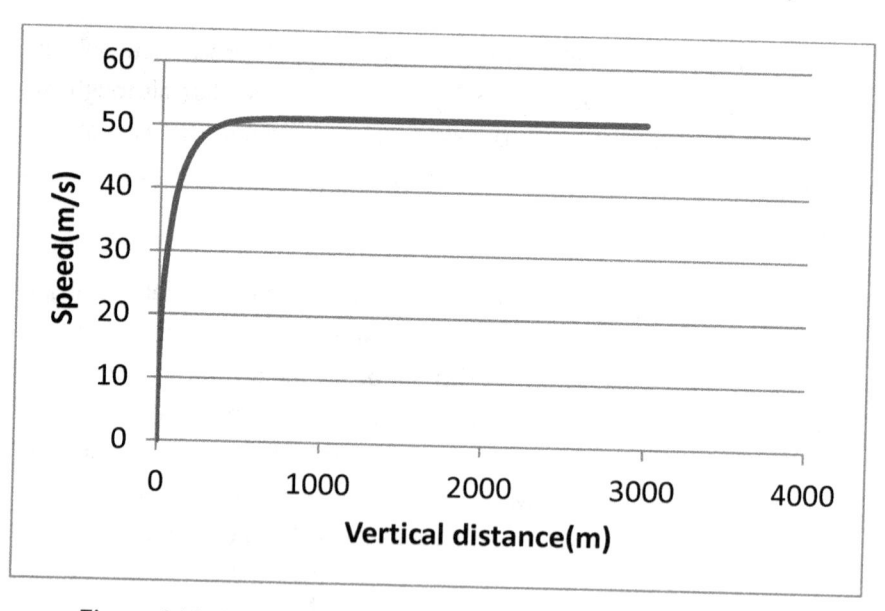

Figure 4.11: Speed variation from a free fall in the atmosphere

A special version of skydiving is the, so called, speed skydiving[16]. In this sport the winner is the athlete that manages to achieve the highest speed. By wearing special costumes and helmets and by maneuvering their bodies, contestants are able to reach speeds higher than 500km/hr. This sport surely is the fastest without the use of a motor.

Finally, it should be noted that for reasons of simplicity, I have assumed that both the density of the air and the acceleration of gravity are constant during the fall. In actual fact both quantities will vary with height.

Rotational kinetic energy

A body may also possess kinetic energy due to rotational motion. It is reminded that when a body rotates, the equivalent to mass is the moment of inertia and the equivalent of speed is angular speed. The formula for kinetic energy due to rotation is thus:

$$E_{kin} = \frac{1}{2} I \Omega^2$$

In the previous chapter we estimated, from the angular speed of the gymnastics athlete at the lowest point of his trajectory for a giant circle, the centripetal force that acts on him at that point. By applying the principle of conservation of mechanical energy (assuming any losses as negligible), we can now see exactly how this angular speed is calculated.

If the center of gravity of the athlete is moving in a circle of radius R, at the highest point, and assuming that his angular speed at this point is zero, his mechanical energy will be equal to $2Rmg$. At the lowest point of the trajectory, if we assume that his potential energy is zero[17], the

---

[16] See, http://www.speedskydiving.eu/
[17] The potential energy can be measured with respect to any height, not only with respect to the ground.

mechanical energy is simply equal to the kinetic energy due to the rotational motion. We thus have:

$$2Rmg = \frac{1}{2}I\Omega^2$$

From the above equation and with some simple algebra we can show that:

$$\Omega^2 = \frac{4Rmg}{I}$$

Assuming that the mass of the athlete is 60kg, the radius of the circle 1m and the moment of inertia 70kgm², we find that:

$$\Omega^2 = 33.63 \frac{rad^2}{s^2}$$

By calculating the square root of 33.63, either by the scientific method of..trial and error, or by pressing the "sqrt" button on our calculator, we find Ω = 5.8rad/s.

The initial source of energy

We have seen the way in which athletes are able to transform one form of energy to another, as for example in a jump when kinetic energy is transformed into potential energy. What though is the initial source of energy for a human being? The answer of course lies with the food that he/she consumes and the calories that it contains.

If we suppose that an athlete consumes 3000Kcal per day, what will be the average power that is produced? In units of Joule this energy is

3000*4184, i.e., almost 12552000. One day has 24*60*60 = 86400s. The average power is thus 12552000/86400 = 145.3W, roughly that produced by two light bulbs. The maximum power that a human can produce over short periods can actually be a few times larger than this. Athletes of course follow a special diet in order to cope with these high energy demands. The great American swimmer Michael Phelps, when training, apparently consumes 12000Kcal per day!

Chapter 5: Various sport projectiles

In physics, when an object is launched in the air it is called a *projectile*. Many of the most popular sports, in one way or another involve the launch of an object. Events such as the shot put, the hammer, the javelin and the discus throw, etc., are the first that come to mind. In many other sports though, where throwing a body as far as possible may not be the ultimate goal, various types of projectiles also play an important role. A free kick in football, a tennis serve, or a three point shot in basketball, also adhere to the physical laws governing projectile motion. Humans themselves can also become projectiles. In the long jump for example, the athlete takes a run up in order to be propelled as far as possible.

In this chapter we will discover which parameters affect the trajectory of a projectile and how competitors are able to tune these in order to improve their performance.

The simplest case

We will begin our analysis with an ideal situation one which, although it contains many simplifications, will give us a good idea of the physical mechanisms determining projectile motion. Let us suppose that we launch a body with an inclination to the ground, and that it follows a curved path that ends up at the same height from which it was launched (see figure 5.1). Let us also suppose that the only force acting on it is its weight.

The first assumption could for example hold for a cross in football or for a golf drive in a course without any inclination. As far as the second assumption is concerned, any object moving in the atmosphere will also experience aerodynamic forces (we have already mentioned some of those), so in order for the assumption to actually hold we should be playing football or golf somewhere in outer space. Nevertheless, the heavier and the less aerodynamic the design of the body is, the smaller the error that this assumption produces. So the trajectory of a shot put is mainly determined by its weight whereas the path of a javelin is greatly affected by the aerodynamic forces.

By making the above assumptions we launch our projectile with an initial speed and inclination. These are the two parameters that the athlete can tune before each attempt.

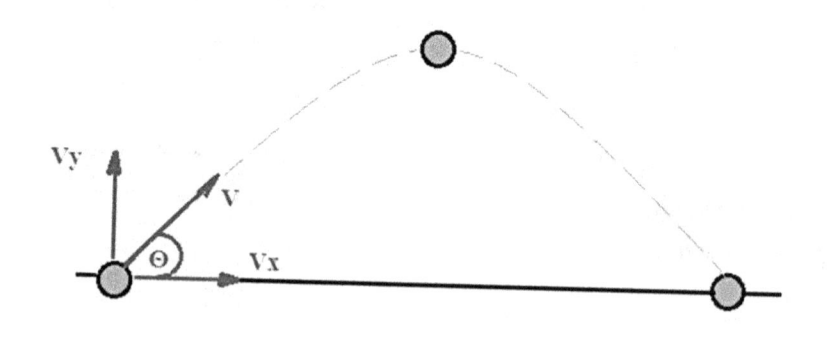

Figure 5.1: Parabolic trajectory of a projectile

A fundamental question that must be addressed is the following: Assuming that the projectile starts off with a speed (V), what should the initial inclination (θ) be, in order to maximise the horizontal distance covered? To answer this, we must carefully consider what is happening during the motion of the body.

What makes things easier is that in physics, if it suits us, we can study this type of motion as the combination of two independent ones. In our case, taking into account that the only force present is the weight of the body, it is convenient to think that the projectile is simultaneously following a horizontal and vertical path.

In order to apply this method, we must divide the initial speed into to two components (as we say in physics), one horizontal and one vertical. This, for those of us that have knowledge of basic mathematics, can easily be achieved by use of trigonometry (a field of mathematics). For our level of analysis it is sufficient to know that the projectile starts off with a horizontal speed which we call V_x and a vertical one V_y. The values of both components (as trigonometry tells us) depend on the initial inclination (θ).

No force acts in the horizontal direction and so according to Newton's second law, the body will maintain a constant speed V_x. In the vertical direction the weight acts opposite to the initial vertical velocity V_y. The vertical motion is exactly the same as that that would occur if we had launched the body vertically upwards. The object will reach a maximum height and then, due to the effect of the weight, will return to its starting point.

The complete trajectory is a combination of the horizontal and vertical ones previously described. Just imagine that we are throwing an object vertically upwards but at the same time we are giving it a constant velocity rightwards. The result would be a curved trajectory, like the one seen in figure 5.1, a trajectory that physicists call a *parabola*.

We have still not answered though our fundamental question, i.e. what the initial inclination must be in order to maximise the range. The strict proof requires knowledge of advanced mathematics; we can also use common sense though to reach the right conclusion. The range is dependent on two factors: on how fast the projectile is travelling horizontally and on how long it can stay in the air. The former requires a large speed V_x, and the latter, a large V_y. For a fixed total speed V, we must make a compromise, since increasing one of the two, implies a decrease in the other. The best combination we can have is to make both speed components equal. Basic trigonometry and common sense tell us that this will happen at an inclination of 45deg. So if you are playing golf somewhere with no atmosphere, on a course without any inclination, so that both our initial assumptions will hold, give the ball an initial inclination of 45deg in order to have the advantage.

A little more realism

Unfortunately for the time being golf competitions are not possible in outer space, so we must introduce a touch of realism. First of all, in most sports that incorporate some kind of throw, the final height of the projectile will be different to the initial one. This occurs since the arms of the athlete are themselves at some distance from the ground. Such a case is the shot put event, a convenient example to use, since, due to the large weight of the shot (7.26kg for men, 4kg for women) and its shape, the aerodynamic forces can be assumed negligible. The trajectory of a put is presented in figure 5.2.

The difference between this case and the one depicted in the previous figure is that the projectile spends more time in the air, as it does not return to its launch height but at a height h meters lower. This allows us to increase the horizontal speed component in relation to the vertical one, in other words to decrease the initial inclination.

Chapter 5: Various sport projectiles

Figure 5.2: Trajectory of a shot

By use of some mathematical calculations we can show that for an initial speed of 13m/s (typical for this event), if the launch takes place 2.1m above the ground (the participants are usually..giants), the ideal initial inclination will be 42deg and the maximum range 19.2m (see figure 5.3).

We observe that even if just slightly we have moved away from the "ideal" 45deg. In reality the shift will be greater. Due to the anatomy of the human arm, at smaller inclinations, a larger speed can be given to the shot, so there is a further tendency towards smaller angles. In order to study this effect I have created a simulation for estimating the range for various launch angles, using a simple model devised by Lithorne[18].

In figure 5.4, I present the variation in launch speed for various initial inclinations.

---

[18] See publication, Lithorne N. P., "Throwing and jumping for maximum horizontal range" (2006), The Physics Teacher, Vol. 38.

73

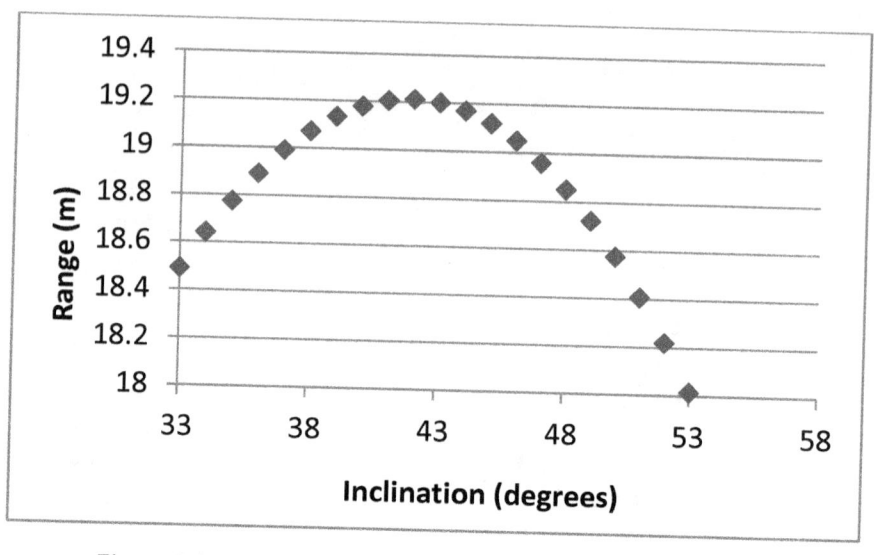

Figure 5.3: Variation of range for various initial inclinations

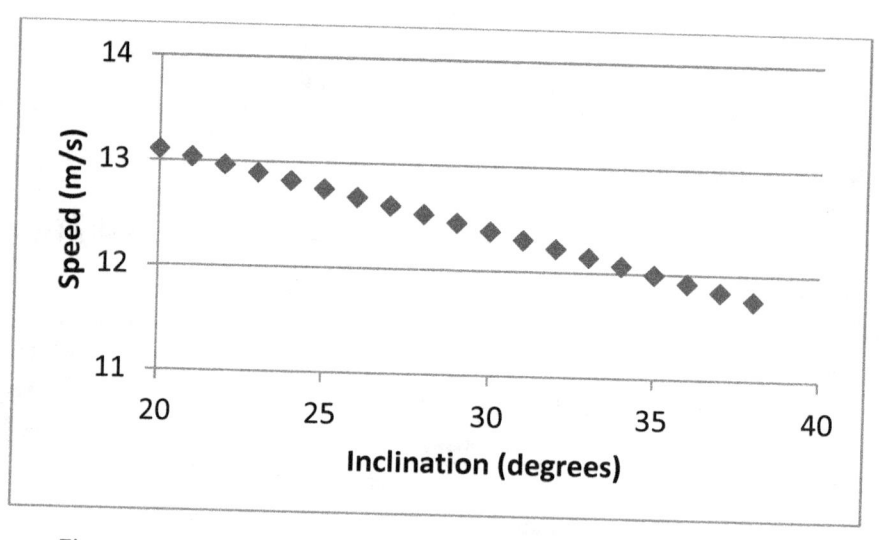

Figure 5.4: Variation of launch speed for various initial inclinations

We see that for greater angles, the launch speed that the athlete can achieve falls below 12m/s.

The effect of the above on the maximum range and ideal launch angle is presented in figure 5.5.

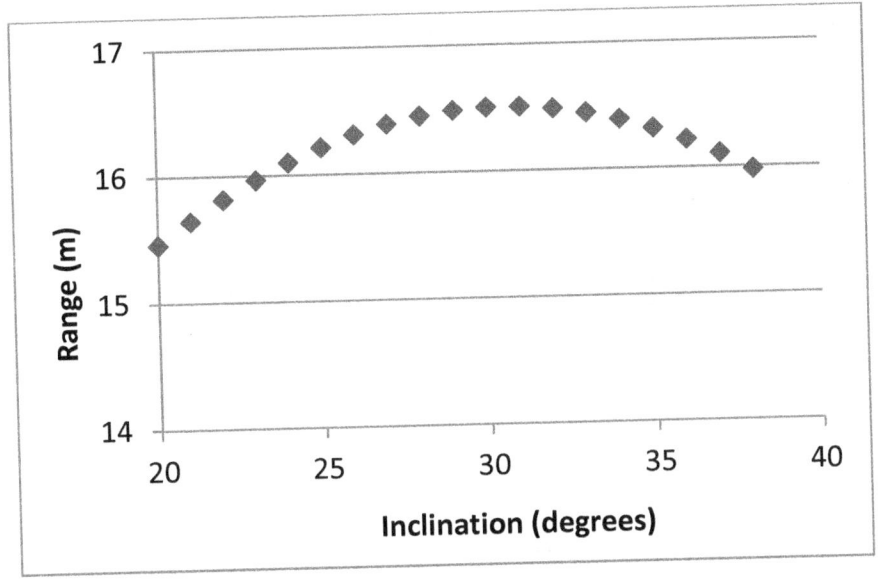

Figure 5.5: Range variation taking into account the arm anatomy

We see that since the athlete cannot maintain a launch speed of 13m/s at larger angles, the maximum range drops to 16.5m. The ideal launch angle also drops to about 31deg.

In the shot put example we have only taken into account the weight of the shot to calculate its trajectory. For many objects, due to their small mass but also to their shape, it is necessary to take into account the effect of the forces that appear due to the interaction of the object with the atmosphere (aerodynamic forces). This, just as the effect of climate conditions (especially wind), requires a separate analysis that will be performed in the next chapter.

Humans in orbit

There are some sports in which the human being, or more correctly the centre of gravity of the athlete, will follow a parabolic orbit. The long jump is such an example. We know that by changing the shape of their body, athletes can shift the position of their centre of gravity. This is exploited in the way seen in figure 5.6.

Figure 5.6: Centre of gravity shift in the long jump

It is clear that due to the different posture of the athlete at the start of the jump the centre of gravity is positioned h meters higher than at touchdown. The trajectory will be more similar to the one described for the shot put and so the flight time and thus the range will be greater than if the centre of gravity ended up at the same height at which it started. Mathematical calculations show us that the difference in range can be quite substantial.

So what is the launch angle the athlete must have in order to maximise the range? From the simple theory of projectiles we would not expect it to be much smaller than 45deg. Measurements have shown us though that the athletes jump at an inclination of about 20deg, i.e. almost half the expected value.

Just like in the shot put, the answer is related to human anatomy. The maximum launch speed that an athlete can achieve depends on the launch angle. For smaller angles, the athlete will lose in range if we see it from the point of view of simple projectile theory, but he will actually gain more due to the increase in launch speed. This is why the ideal launch angle is smaller than expected. It becomes clear that in many sports, human anatomy is the determining factor for the right launch angles.

Does Michael Jordan Fly?

Arguably the greatest basketball player of all time, Michael Jordan's leaps towards the basket rings have become legendary, giving him the nickname "Air Jordan". The sensation given to spectators was that he actually floated and at times almost stood in the air. Was all of this just an illusion generated from the enthusiasm of the crowd, or can it be explained by the laws of physics?

As Jordan "flies" towards the ring, he must obey the laws of projectiles, so we would expect him to follow a parabolic orbit. We know now though that what actually follows a parabola is the centre of gravity of the athlete. The rest of his body parts can move differently as long as the "mean" trajectory is parabolic. So if Jordan changes his shape by lifting his arms and legs, then his head could, for a short time, remain at a constant height. As our focus is usually on his head, we have the illusion that the whole athlete "stands" in mid air.

Measurements on ballet dancers that perform similar acts, have confirmed the above. If you still find this hard to believe, just throw a hammer. Although the centre of gravity of the hammer follows a parabolic trajectory, its head will move in a more complex way.

Projectiles and accuracy

In the sports that we have examined so far, we were primarily interested in maximising the range. In many cases though it is the accuracy and not the distance that is more crucial.

An Introduction To The Physics Of Sports

Such an example is basketball. The success of a shot depends to a great extent on the angle with which the ball reaches the ring. The smaller the angle, the less of the ring is seen by the ball. Researchers have shown that the minimum approach angle for a successful shot is about 32deg.

The approach angle, the launch angle and the initial ball speed as it leaves the athlete's hand, are all related to each other according to the laws of projectiles. So for example, if we assume that the ball is only under the effect of its weight, the launch angle and the initial speed are related in the way depicted in figure 5.7. This graph has been created for a free throw shot (4.57m from the ring) and a launch height 0.9m below the ring.

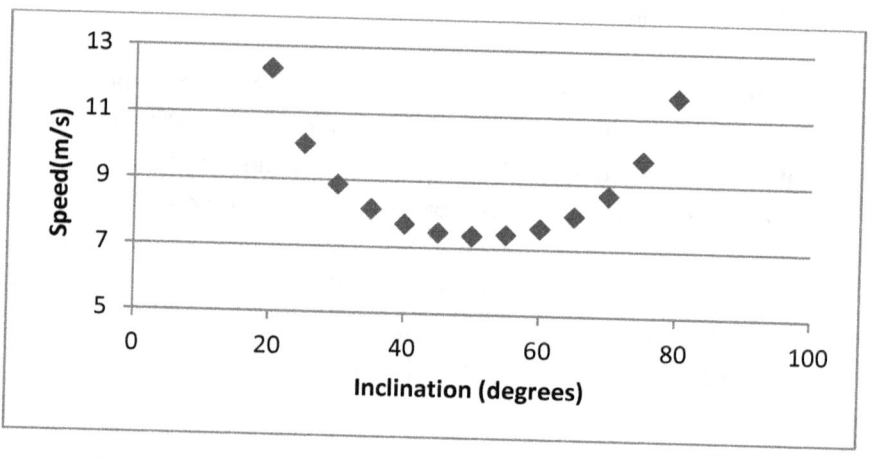

Figure 5.7: Launch angle and initial speed for a free throw

It usually suits us to restrict the speed to low values, so that if the ball hits the ring, it still has a chance of entering it. From the above graph, in order to minimise the speed we must use a launch angle of just over 50deg.

The best players can control the launch angle to an accuracy of +-1 degree. The error in launch angle will appear as a deviation in the final position of the ball in relation to the ring. Mathematical calculations can show that the deviation caused will increase with increased launch angle.

Chapter 5: Various sport projectiles

By taking all of the above into consideration researchers have shown that the ideal launch angles lie between 50-55 degrees. By adding spin to the ball the chances of success increase as the path will become more stable and the ball will also acquire the correct direction if it hits the ring. Of course other factors, not at all negligible, such as the position of the defenders' hands, will also affect the shooter's decisions.

For a clearer picture I have created a simulation of the trajectory of a basketball for a free throw. The free throw line, as I have already mentioned, is positioned at 4.57m from the ring that is at a height of 3.05m. We assume that the ball leaves the hands of the athlete at a speed of 7.5m/s and at an inclination of 52deg. To be more realistic, we take into account the air resistance and the Magnus force acting upwards, as we have given the ball a spin of 13Hz. The results are provided in figure 5.8[19].

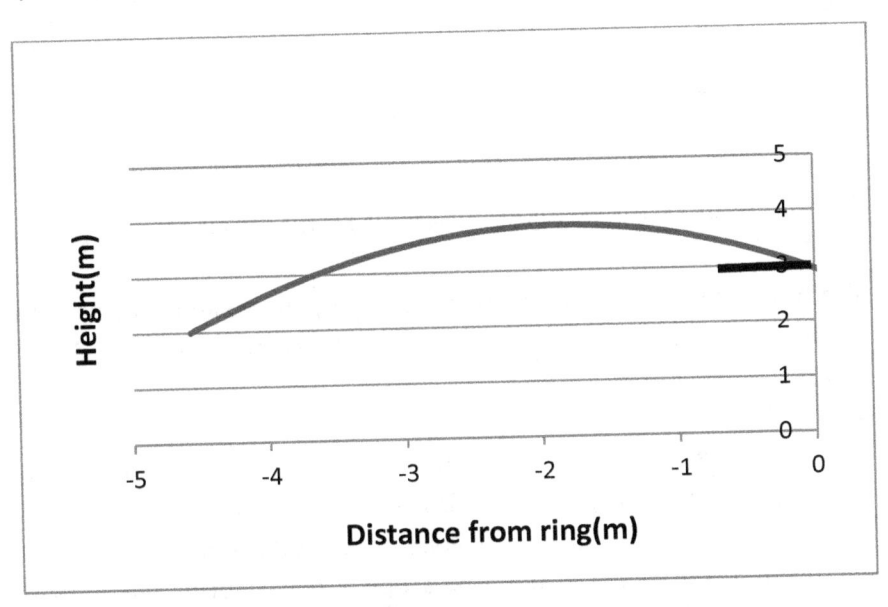

Figure 5.8: Ball trajectory after a free throw

---

[19] For reasons related to the mathematical modelling, we assume the displacement to the left of the ring to be negative.

The shot is successful as the ball ends up almost in the center of the ring. It is interesting also to observe the variation of the inclination of the ball's trajectory (see figure 5.9), as we know that a condition for success is that the approach angle should be greater than 32deg.

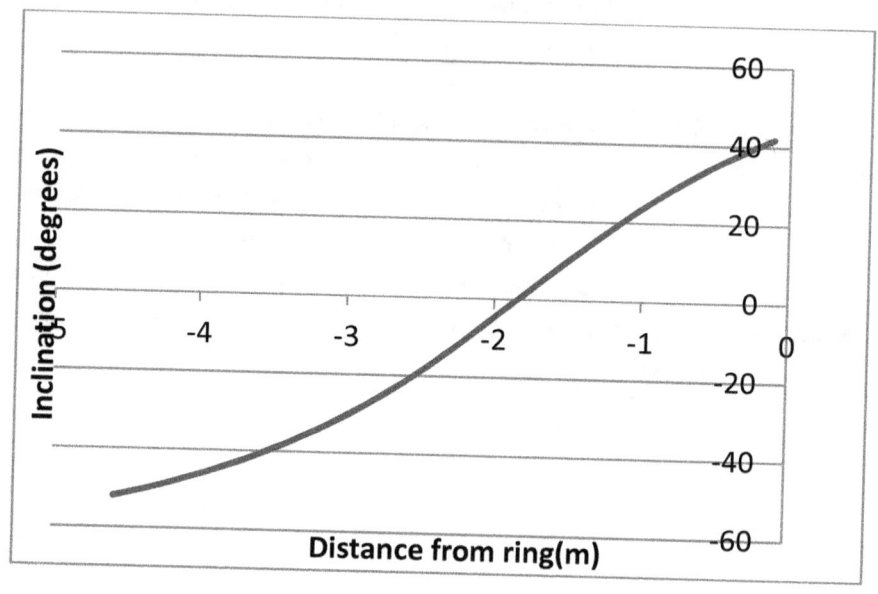

Figure 5.9: Ball trajectory inclination after a free throw

The ball starts with an inclination of 52deg (upwards) and ends up with a positive inclination (downwards) of 43deg, greater than the 32deg that is the lower limit.

Finally in figure 5.10 we can view the trajectory of the ball if the aerodynamic forces are ignored. The final position is about 15cm further behind, hitting the ring instead of going through its centre. The conclusion from a mathematical modeling scope is that ignoring the aerodynamic forces will introduce a small error to our calculations. Whether this error is considered important or not depends on the objectives of the simulation.

Chapter 5: Various sport projectiles

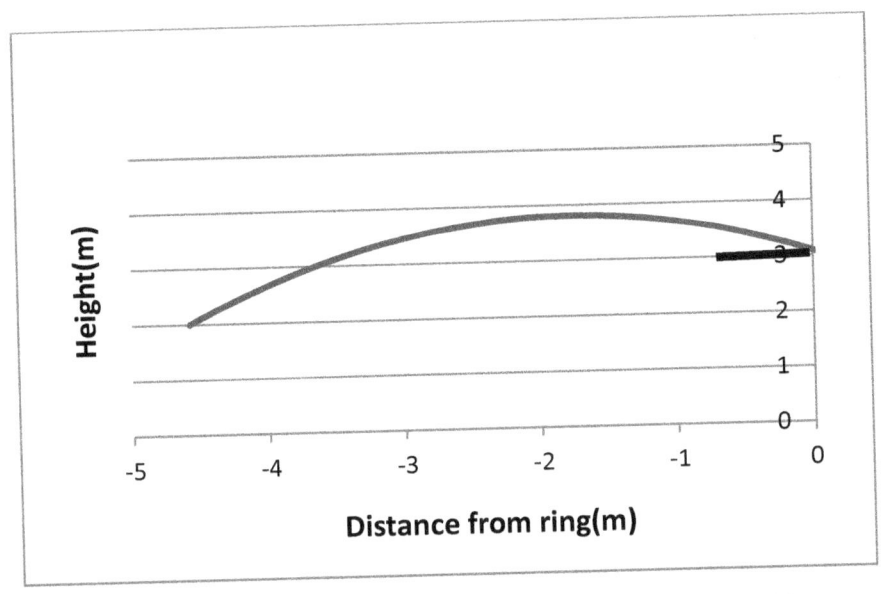

Figure 5.10: Ball trajectory without aerodynamic forces

We will leave basketball with an interesting thought. From a purely statistical point of view, it is worth shooting a two pointer rather than a three pointer, if the chances of scoring are more than 1.5 times greater (as a three pointer is worth 1.5 times a two point shot). Let us assume that a player has a 45% success rate for shots taken from a position closer than the free throw line. On the other hand, for shots taken just outside the three point line he has a 30% chance of success. It therefore seems that shots taken between the free throw line and the three point line have less than 1.5 times the chance of success than those taken outside 7.25m. One could conclude that taking shots in this region is not to the player's advantage. Statistics of course do not always tell the truth.

There are other examples where accuracy and not distance is more important in a sport. This is the case for tennis serve, where the player must hit the ball so that it clears the net (of height roughly 1 meter[20]) and lands in an area of 26.33m².

---

[20] The height of the net varies between 0.914m at its centre to 1.07m at the ends.

The margin (or window) of error in the tennis serve launch angle depends on the launch height, the ball speed and the spin. The larger the height, the larger the margin of error that will allow for a successful serve. It has been calculated that for a 90mile/hr serve, increasing the launch height from 85 inches to 105 inches, roughly doubles the chances of success. Tall players have an advantage here as well.

Increasing speed will decrease the error margin. For example, if we hit the ball at a height of 85 inches, a speed of 120miles/hr instead of 90miles/hr will decrease the chance of success by three times. On the other hand of course, increasing the serve speed will make life more difficult for our opponent. Finally, by adding topspin to the ball, we can almost double our chances.

Shot accuracy naturally plays an important role in football. In the European Championships of 2012 (Euro 2012), the Greek national team had an excellent run, reaching the quarter finals of the tournament. By careful study of the official statistics as published by UEFA, one notices something strange[21]. Although the team managed to finish in the top eight teams of the competition, the positions it is placed in according to the statistical markers are much lower. To illustrate this I have created the following table.

Game aspect	Position
Average goals scored	8th
Average goals against	15th
Ball possession	15th
Attempts on target	16th
Attempts off target	14th
Corners	15th
Passes attempted	10th

Table 5.1: Position of Greece in several aspects of the game in the Euro 2012

---

[21] See my article: "The Greek Paradox at Euro 2012", at the web page http://www.significancemagazine.org/details/webexclusive/2206091/The-Greek-paradox-at-Euro-2012.html.

It is indicative, that apart from the number of goals scored in each game, in all other aspects Greece lies outside the top eight positions. So how did the team manage to qualify to the quarter finals? Luck of course does play a role, as does the ability to win important games. In the last game of the group stages Greece had to beat Russia, with any other result it would have been eliminated and most probably ended up last in the group. By winning the game 1-0, Greece managed to surpass its opponents.

Do any statistics exist then, that would justify the successful run of the team? In the following table, I present the percentage of attempts at goal that were successful (i.e. ended in a goal scored).

Team	Percentage (%)
Greece	17.9
Denmark	14.8
Sweden	13.9
England	13.9
Germany	13.3
Croatia	13.3
Spain	13.0
Czech Republic	10.8
Russia	10.2
Portugal	7.5
Italy	5.6
Ukraine	5.3
France	4.8
Poland	4.5
Ireland	4.0
Netherlands	3.7

Table 5.2: Percentage of successful attempts in the Euro 2012

What we observe is that, by quite a margin, Greece is the team with the greatest accuracy percentage. The team needed fewer attempts in order to score a goal. It may be that this accuracy was a crucial component for its success.

Chapter 6: Aerodynamics in sport

In the previous chapter we studied sports that incorporated the flight of an object (or a human) in the air. The cases discussed in more detail were those where the object weight played the greatest role in the trajectory determination. When the *aerodynamic* forces, i.e. those forces related to the interaction of an object with the air, are more important, then a different type of analysis is required. This analysis will be performed in this chapter.

Basic aerodynamics concepts

Any object in flight will experience forces due to its interaction with the atmosphere. These so called aerodynamic forces are the ones that make airline travel around the world possible. The wings of an airplane for example, are designed in such a way, so that their relative to the atmosphere motion creates a force that opposes gravity, thus keeping the airplane from falling. This force is *lift*, due to which the distances between countries have been reduced drastically during the last 100 years. On the other hand, in order for the aircraft to move horizontally, it requires a thrust force from its engine so that it can overcome the air resistance, another aerodynamic force that aeronautical engineers call *drag*.

All human inventions in the field of flight in one way or another, exploit this interaction with the air. A helicopter for example, that is in hover, i.e. stationary above a certain area, uses its main rotor to push the air downwards. By doing so, and according to Newton's 3rd law, the action-reaction one, the helicopter itself experiences an upward force, a kind of lift that balances its weight and keeps it in the air.

So anything that flies, is under the influence of two types of forces, the gravitational ones (i.e. weight) and the aerodynamic ones (if an engine exists then we must also include the thrust forces). The direction and magnitude of these forces determine the path of the object, just like in the case of the flight of a football leaving the foot of a player. The time has now come to find out more about the aerodynamic forces.

Drag

Drag is the more scientific term for what we have up to this point called air resistance. It is the force that we feel decelerating us when we are cycling, or pulling our hand back whenever we stick it out of a window of a moving car. As we have discussed, both in the cycling example and for the motion of a football, the effect of drag is always decelerating.

It can be shown that drag is proportional to the body surface area, to air density (which decreases at higher altitudes) and to the square of the speed of the body. The fact that it is proportional to the square of speed, tells us that if the speed is doubled then drag will increase by four times, so the effect is very considerable. We can summarise all of the above in a mathematical formula:

$$D = \frac{1}{2} \rho A V^2 C_D$$

Where:
ρ is air density,
A is the surface area of the body,
V is the speed relative to the air,
C_D is the drag coefficient.

The *drag coefficient* is a pure number (with no units), that is related to the aerodynamic design of an object. For the wings of an aircraft, for which we require minimum air resistance, C_D will be somewhere in the order of 0.05. On the other hand, for footballs, which were never designed for transatlantic flights, the value of C_D after a free kick will be around 0.2, i.e. about four times larger. We know that the air density at low altitudes is about 1.2kg/m³, the diameter of a ball is 0.22m and the speed given to the ball by a strong player can reach 30m/s, so we estimate the drag to be[22]:

$$D = \frac{1}{2}\rho A V^2 C_D = \frac{1}{2} 1.2 \left(\frac{\pi 0.22^2}{4} \right) 30^2 0.2 = 4.1N$$

On the other hand the weight of a ball (that has a mass of 0.43kg) is given by:

$$W = mg = 0.43 \cdot 9.81 = 4.2N$$

It is evident that the drag force is of the same order of magnitude as the weight, and will have to be taken into account if we wish to determine the trajectory of the ball accurately. The same, as we will see, applies to many other sports.

The degree of the air resistance effect can be anticipated by the fact that if a player shoots a football with a speed of 35m/s (probably about the highest speed achievable) and with a launch angle of 45deg, it will

---

[22] The surface of area of a sphere is given by its diameter D according to $\pi D^2/4$.

travel for about **65m** until hitting the ground. If the same shot was taken in an environment with no drag (a vacuum), then the distance travelled would become 125m. Football pitches in outer space would have to have very large dimensions. On the other hand, due to this force, the speed of tennis balls will decrease by about 25% by the time they reach the opponent on the other side of the court. A table tennis ball would not even make it to the net of a tennis court.

The drag force is generated by more than one physical mechanism. Thus, the total drag is made up of various types, depending on each type's source. At this stage we will focus on the following two: The first is called *friction* or *surface drag*, and is created due of the friction between the molecules of the air and the surface of the body and due of the friction between the layers of the air itself. To understand this just think of how honey runs when you put it on a plate. The part of the honey that is in contact with the plate surface moves very slowly. The layers near the surface are also affected by the slow motion of the first layer. As we move further away from the plate the smaller the effect and the higher the speed of the honey. The area near the body surface where the flow is decelerated is called the *boundary layer*. By making surfaces smoother, we can decrease the friction drag, which is actually more important for aircraft wings than for most sports.

The type of drag that has a greater influence on most sports is *pressure drag*. This force is generated from the presence of the body in the air flow which creates a difference in pressure between the front and rear sides, as seen in the following figure.

We can see that behind the ball an area of vortices and lower pressure is created. In aerodynamics this area is called a *wake*. In this way, the pressure on the front of the ball is greater, creating a resultant force (drag) opposing the motion of the ball. What is interesting is that if a critical speed is surpassed, then the wake (for reasons that we will not go into but are related to the change in the flow of the air) decreases

Chapter 6: Aerodynamics in sport

in size and so does the pressure difference. So at a certain speed the value of the drag drops suddenly (the phenomenon is known as *drag crisis*). For a football this will occur at about 15m/s.

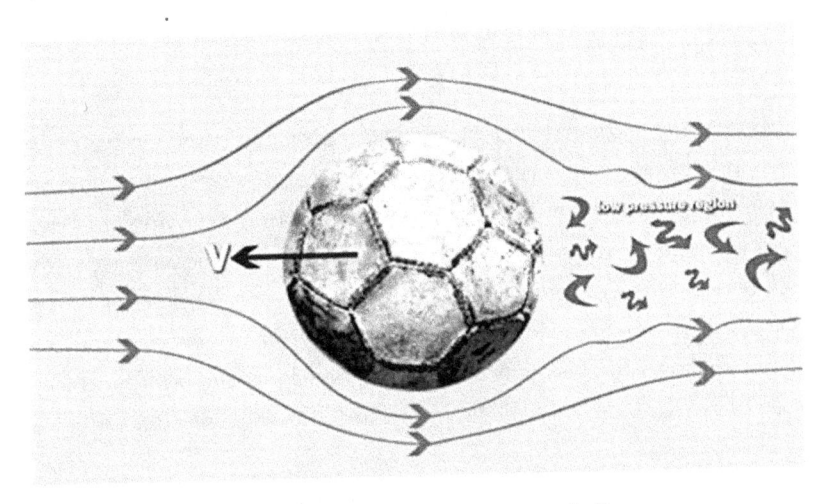

Figure 6.1: Pressure drag on a ball

The critical speed at which the wake shrinks and pressure drag drops depends on how smooth the body surface is. So although that for friction drag, smoother surfaces were preferred, it turns out that for rougher surfaces the pressure drag decreases at a lower speed, i.e. the critical speed is smaller. This is the reason that golf balls have dimples. In this way the critical speed is achieved faster and the total drag during the ball flight is reduced, thus increasing the range. Finally, pressure drag increases when the surface area of the body exposed to the flow is increased. This is the motivation behind the posture of cyclists during a race. It is also why in the year 2000, the International Table Tennis Federation increased the ball size (from a diameter of 38mm to 40mm) in order to slow the game down.

Lift

For bodies with aerodynamic shapes another effect of the air comes into play, this time as a force perpendicular to the motion path. Physicists call this force *lift*.

Although many explanations of lift have been published, some of which are wrong, my own view is that the simplest and easiest to understand is the following: As the air hits the body, for example a wing, its flow follows the shape of the wing which deflects the flow downwards (the so called, *downwash*). The change in the flow direction (and so in its velocity), appears when the wing is curved (*cambered*, in aeronautical terms), or if it is inclined to the air flow. This inclination of the wing, and for that matter of any object to an air flow, is called the *angle of attack*.

According to Newton's 1st law, if the velocity of the air changes (in direction) due to the wing presence, the wing must be exerting a force on it. According to the 3rd law (action-reaction again), the air must also be exerting a force on the wing. To sum it up, we can say that the cause of lift is this: The air flow changes direction due to the presence of the wing, so as a reaction, the air exerts a force on the wing itself (see figure 6.2).

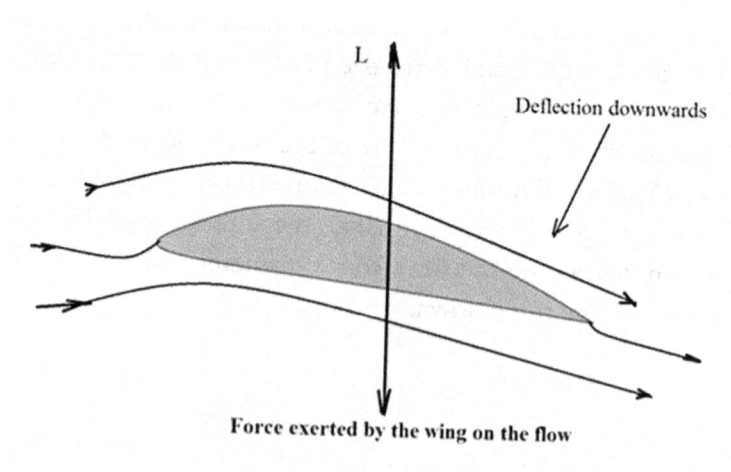

Figure 6.2: Creation of lift

The formula giving lift is:

$$L = \frac{1}{2}\rho V^2 A C_L$$

We notice that it is very similar to the one for drag, something expected as both forces are related to the air flow. The coefficient C_L is the *lift coefficient* and depends on the shape of the body and the angle of attack, i.e. its inclination to the flow. As we will see below, lift plays an important role in the performance of athletes competing in events such as the discus and javelin throw. Spherical objects on the other hand do not possess good aerodynamic properties and the lift they create is considered negligible.

It should be emphasised that in the formulas for lift and drag the speed *V* is the speed that is relative to the air and not with respect to the ground. The importance of this will be revealed in the next chapter.

Magnus force

Some of the most impressive shots taken in a football game are produced by applying spin to the ball. The members of the Brazilian national team were the first to use this technique for free kicks, exciting the crowds by scoring difficult goals. Since then almost all free kicks that are taken just outside the penalty box are executed in this way, helping the player to give the ball a curved trajectory, thus clearing the defensive wall and beating the goalkeeper.

So what is this force that is responsible for the deflection of the ball? The first to engage himself with the study of this phenomenon was, who else, but Isaac Newton, who tried to provide an explanation for the curved paths of tennis balls (a sport particularly popular during his time). Those however who reached solid scientific conclusions were

An Introduction To The Physics Of Sports

Rayleigh and Magnus in 1842, who analysed the deflection in the path of cannon balls that spun round themselves. What they realised was that the force responsible for their curved path (and also the force that affects a football trajectory), is related to the interaction between the spinning object and the air that surrounds it. So it is yet another aerodynamic force, this time present only when an object is spinning.

As we see in the following figure, the rotational motion of the ball drags the air around it, so changing the direction of its flow. This, once again as a result of the action-reaction law, results in a force being exerted on the ball itself. So a ball turning clockwise, like the one seen in the figure, will feel an upward force.

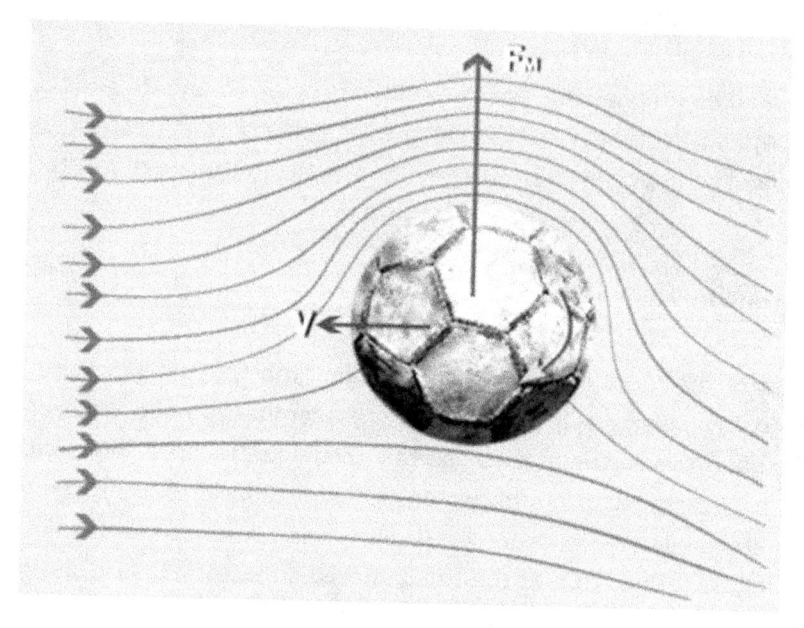

Figure 6.3 Magnus force

As we saw in chapter 2, the formula that gives us the Magnus force for a typical football, can be approximated by:

$$F_M = \pi^2 \rho R^3 Vf = 3.14^2 \cdot 1.2 \cdot 0.11^3 \cdot 30 \cdot 7 = 3.3N$$

Once more, we see that it is of the same order of magnitude as the weight of the ball and can certainly not be ignored.

Aerodynamic sports

Now that we know more about aerodynamic forces, we must find a means of differentiating between those sports where they play an important role and those where weight is the determining factor.

One method for this would be to find the quotient of the drag over the weight and establish for which sports this is relatively large. The following table[23] contains data for some popular sports. The quotients are derived for typical speeds achieved in these sports.

Sport	Quotient of drag/weight
Shot put (women)	0.008
Shot put (men)	0.01
Hammer throw	0.02
Long jump	0.03
Basketball	0.07
Discus throw (men)	0.15
Discus throw (women)	0.28
Ski jumping athlete	0.2-0.3
Javelin throw (men)	0.64
Javelin throw (women)	0.85
Tennis ball	1.00
Football	1.02
Golf ball	1.23
Table tennis ball	8.80

Table 6.1: Quotient of drag/weight

---

[23] For most sports the data was taken from the book: de Mestre N., "The mathematics of projectiles in sport" (1990), Australian Mathematical Society Lecture Series.

We observe that for the first three (shot put, hammer throw, long jump) the values of the quotient are much smaller than for the rest. For these events we can approximately assume that the trajectory of the projectile is determined only by its weight. As the quotient increases so do the aerodynamic effects. It is interesting to note that the tennis ball, football and golf ball, although of different size, have almost the same value of quotient.

Flying with skis

Another sport than can be deemed as aerodynamic is ski jumping, one of the most popular events of the winter Olympic Games. The athlete basically follows five stages during his attempt: the initial downhill (where speed is increased), the takeoff (where the athlete is propelled forward in order to lift off the ground), free flight, landing and deceleration on the ground.

From an aerodynamic point of view, we are more interested in the free flight stage. At this point the athlete acts like an aircraft wing, setting his posture in order to maximise the range. The forces acting on him (and his skis) are drag (D), opposing the motion, lift (L), perpendicular to the motion and weight (W), vertically downwards.

By use of Newton's laws and by making certain simplifications, I have created a mathematical model of the motion of the athlete in the air.

The simulation results are portrayed in figures 6.5 to 6.9 and are for a skier of mass 70kg (this includes his apparatus). The coordinates of the trajectory refer to the takeoff point and in this case are for a jump of 100m in horizontal distance, initial speed of 27m/s, initial inclination with respect to the horizon (γ) 10deg and angle of attack (α) 30deg. We see that for this jump the vertical drop is about 70m, which is of the order of magnitude observed for actual jumps.

Chapter 6: Aerodynamics in sport

Figure 6.4 Forces during a ski jump

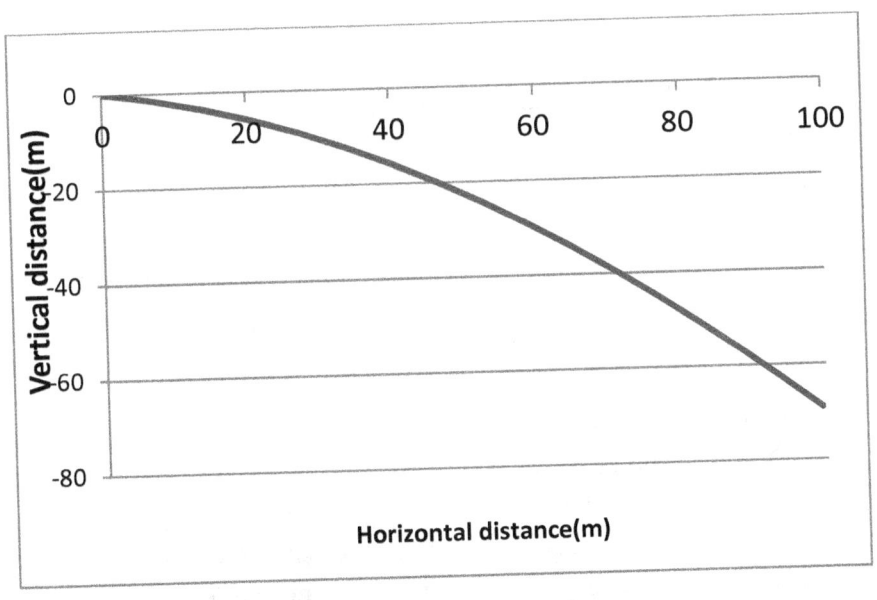

Figure 6.5: Trajectory coordinates

95

In figure 6.6 the variation of speed is presented during the flight. The speed increases due to the effect of gravity, producing a landing value of about 41m/s. This is slightly greater than expected but is still of the same order of magnitude of that found by other researchers.

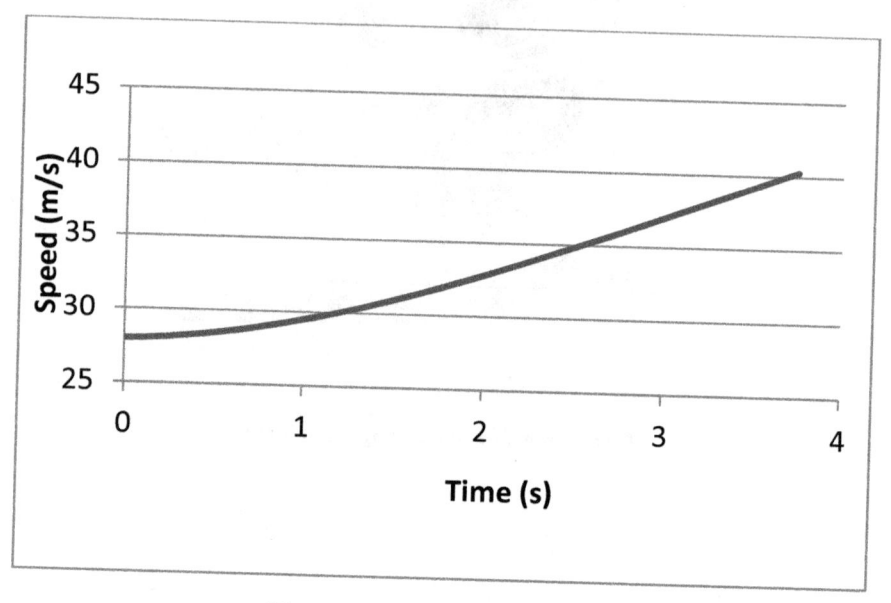

Figure 6.6: Variation of speed

In the next figure the variation of the inclination of the athlete is illustrated, giving a final landing inclination of 49deg. The inclination of the hill is about 36deg, so the landing angle with respect to the ground is 13deg, allowing for a safe landing.

What interests us more though is the effect of the aerodynamic forces, presented in the following diagrams. We see that during the flight they increase due to the increase in speed. We also observe that the values start off from about 12-13% of the weight and reach roughly 25%. This suggests that they significantly influence the path of the athlete and it would be a mistake to ignore them like we did for example, for the shot put.

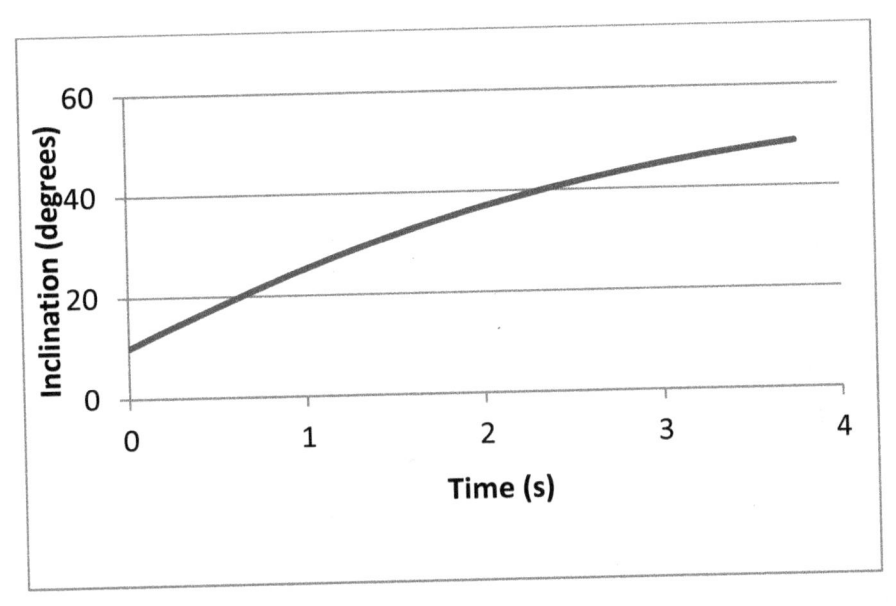

Figure 6.7: Variation of inclination

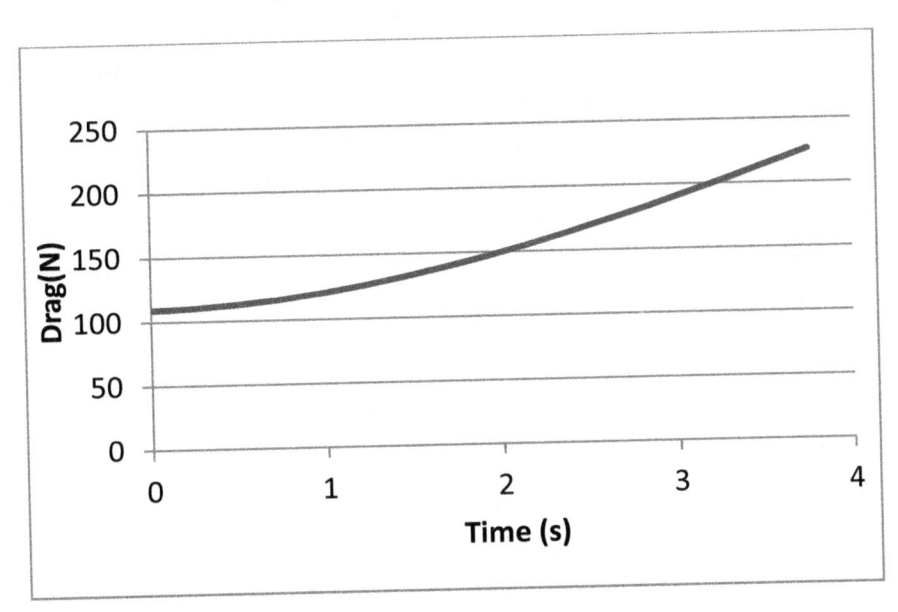

Figure 6.8: Drag variation

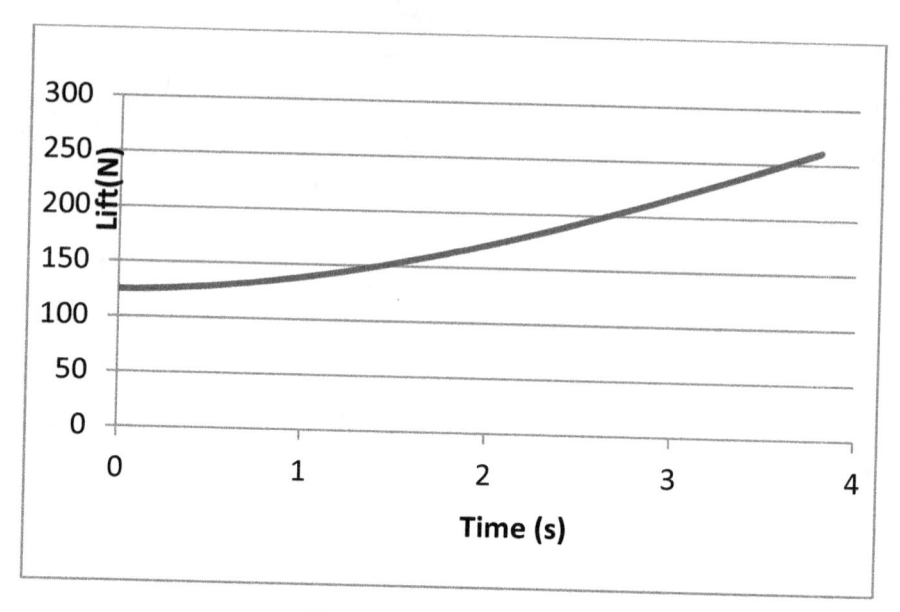

Figure 6.9: Lift variation

We deduce that aerodynamics significantly affect the performance in a ski jump. The posture that the athlete takes, his dress, etc., can determine the final outcome of his attempt. You will have noticed for example, that the technique used by most modern athletes is the so called, V-style, where the athlete opens his legs in a V shape. (see figure 6.10). Many studies have shown that this posture improves the aerodynamic efficiency, resulting in greater range.

Figure 6.10: The V-style tecnique

Javelin aerodynamics

In table 6.1 we note that one of the most aerodynamic sports, is the javelin throw. In fact, the aerodynamic properties of the javelin had to be modified by the IAAF in order to keep the event safe.

What happened was that in 1984 the East German Uwe Hohn broke the world record with a monstrous, 104.8m throw. With this kind of performance there became a danger that the javelin would soon have the same effect for which it was used in ancient years, i.e. the injury of someone. In 1986 this, together with the fact that many throws were invalid (for a valid throw the javelin must land tip first), forced the ruling body to move the center of gravity of the javelin, 4cm forward and to redesign its rear part by making it thinner. Similar changes were made to the women's event in 1999.

So what did this change in design achieve? In order to understand, we must have a look at two of the forces acting on a javelin, as seen in the following figure.

Center of Pressure

Center of Gravity

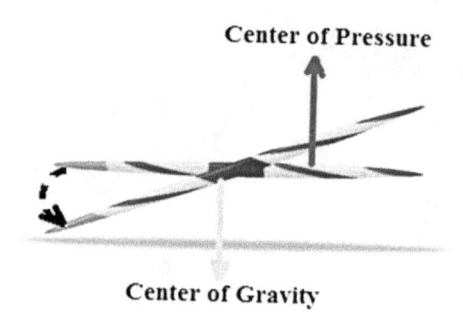

Figure 6.11: Weight and lift acting on a javelin

The lift acts at a point that is known as the *centre of pressure*. We discussed in a previous chapter that when a force F acts at a distance d from a point, then a torque $M=Fd$, is created about that point. This torque puts the body in a rotational motion.

As the centre of pressure *behind* the centre of gravity, the aerodynamic forces will turn the javelin tip downwards. The further forward the centre of gravity is in relation to the centre of pressure, the larger the torque that causes the javelin to turn. This results in a reduced range and on increased chances of a valid throw. By moving the centre of gravity forward designers achieved both their goals.

A problem with the centre of pressure is that it shifts position during the flight. By making the rear of the javelin thinner, it can be shown that the range of centre of pressure positions is reduced, making the trajectory more predictable.

In order to obtain a better idea of the flight of a javelin I created another simple simulation[24]. The mathematical model contains many simplifications, for example the centre of pressure is assumed to be at a constant position during the flight. It does provide us though with realistic results,

---

[24] Most numerical data are from the book White C., «Projectile dynamics in sport» (2010), Routledge, Taylor and Francis.

Chapter 6: Aerodynamics in sport

as seen in the following figures. The initial speed is assumed 30m/s, the initial angle of attack zero degrees and the initial inclination to the horizontal, 30deg. It is also assumed that the javelin is launched 2m from the ground, that the centre of gravity is 0.255m in front of the centre of pressure and that the moment of inertia is 0.42kgm².

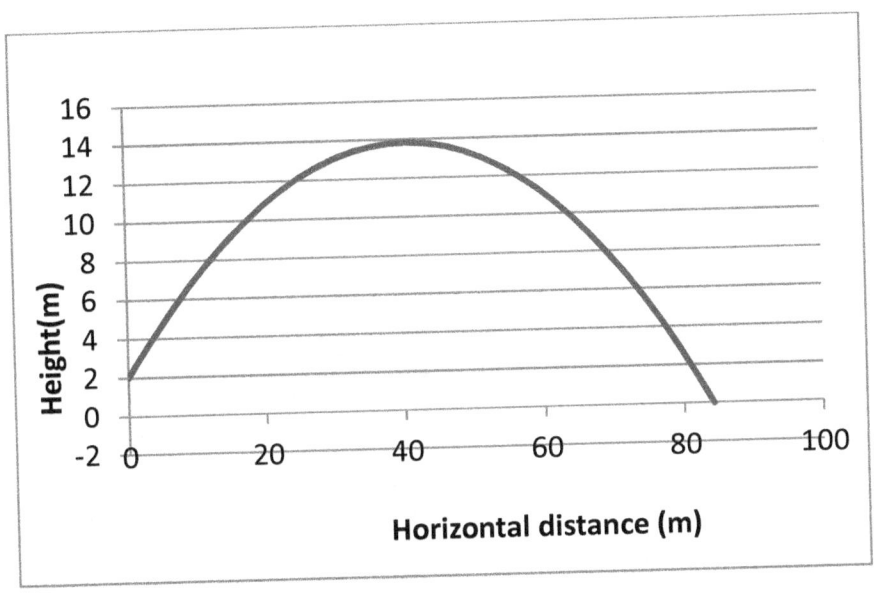

Figure 6.12: Javelin trajectory

We see that a curved path is followed and the javelin travels for about 84m, a pretty good throw. Is it valid though? To check this we must find the inclination as it hits the ground. Since I have assumed that a nose up inclination is positive, for a valid throw, the sign must be negative at landing.

In figure 6.13 we see that (after a bit of wobbling), due to the relative positions of centre of gravity and centre of pressure, the initial inclination of 30deg nose up, starts to decrease and becomes negative after 2.3s. The javelin lands safely with a nose down inclination of about 17deg.

An Introduction To The Physics Of Sports

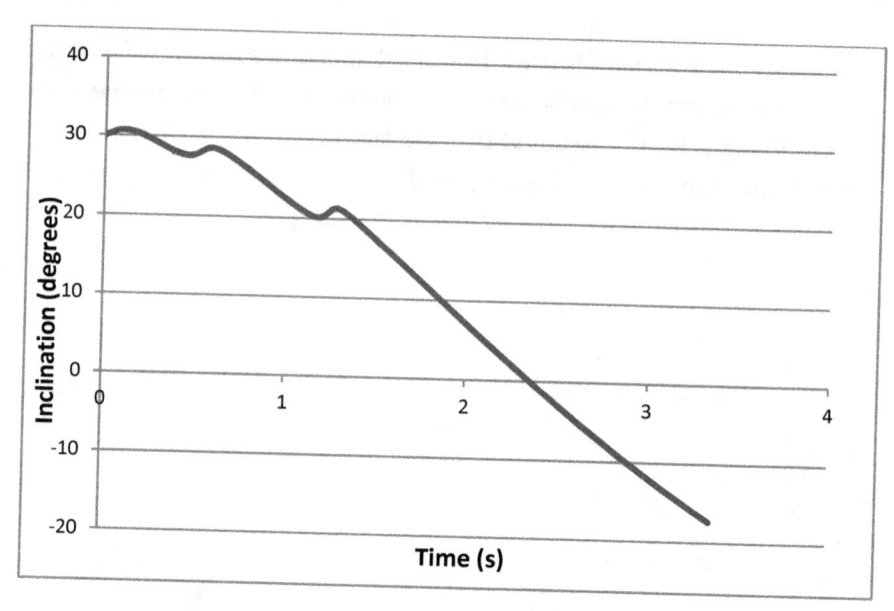

Figure 6.13: Javelin inclination

Hydrodynamics and swimming

The physical mechanisms that determine the motion of a swimmer resemble those that define the trajectory of a body in the air. This occurs since both water and air are *fluids*, i.e. they can flow, constantly changing their shape. It is because of this that the forces generated due to the motion of a body submerged in either, are similar.

The forces acting on a swimmer are presented in figure 6.14.

In the horizontal direction we have the thrust provided by the arms and legs of the swimmer and the water drag, and vertically, the weight and a force of opposite direction, which in hydrodynamics is called the *buoyant* force.

Chapter 6: Aerodynamics in sport

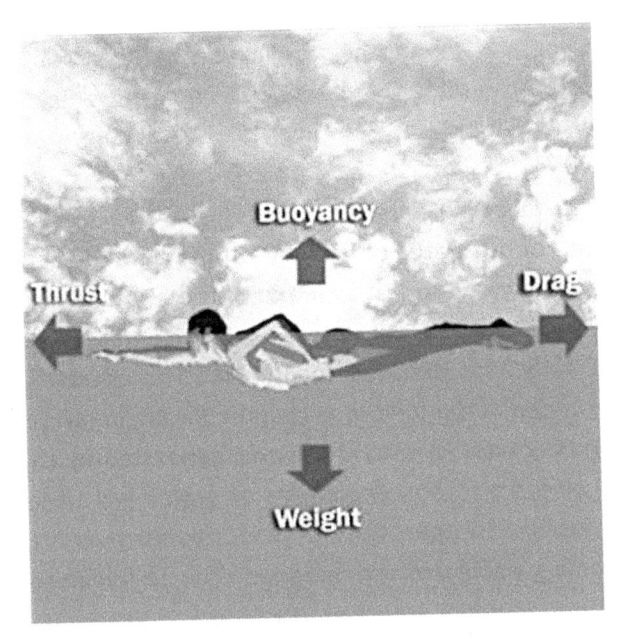

Figure 6.14: Forces acting on a swimmer

The buoyant force is the force that allows us to float in the water. It is created due to the difference in the pressure exerted by the water at different depths. We are all aware of this if we dive under water, as our ears feel the effect. This results in a greater force being exerted on the lower part of a body than on the upper one, producing a net force acting upwards. The overall effect is for the body to be pushed to the surface of the water. The value of the buoyant force depends on the density of the fluid in which the body is submerged. This revelation was enough to make the ancient Greek, Archimedes, leave his bath exclaiming the famous "Eureka". We realise this from the fact that it is easier to float in the sea than in a lake[25].

The athlete produces forward thrust by use of his/her arms and legs. The exact mechanism for thrust generation depends on the swimming style (e.g. breaststroke, backstroke, etc) and the technique of the athlete.

---

[25] The buoyant force also exists in gasses, but due to their lower density will not be as large as in fluids.

103

Broadly speaking, it is yet another application of the action-reaction law. The swimmer pushes the water backwards and the water exerts a force in the forward direction.

The water resistance, i.e. drag, just like in flight is generated mainly due to the collision of the water molecules with the athlete and to the friction between the water and the surface of the body. The first source of drag can be minimised by taking a more horizontal posture, thus decreasing the body area exposed to the flow. The effect of friction will be discussed more in the following chapter. Finally, in swimming, a third form of drag is created due to the waves generated by the motion of the athlete, *wave drag*. The appearance of waves will obstruct the efforts of the athlete. In open water events this form of drag is greater than in swimming pools that are designed so as to minimise the effect.

Chapter 7: Are all records the same?

In the previous chapters a review of the physical laws that determine the performance of athletes was conducted through various examples in sport. It was revealed that apart from those aspects that relate to the abilities of each athlete, such as strength and technique, there exist other factors, mainly environmental, for example wind speed, which will also significantly affect the overall performance.

In this chapter we will study in more detail the effect of those parameters, such as weather conditions, altitude, even the dress of athletes, and will realise that the objective comparison of performances and records is actually harder than we may have imagined.

The assisting wind

Probably the most obvious effect of external factors on athlete performance is that of wind. This is the reason that in many athletics events, such as in sprint events and the long jump, for a record to be officially recognised, it must have been achieved with an assisting wind of less than 2m/s.

Any runner will feel the effect of drag, the value of which depends on the relative speed between the athlete and the air. So if the ground speed of the athlete is V and the speed of an assisting wind V_{wind}, then the relative speed will be $V-V_{wind}$, i.e. less than if the wind speed were zero (still wind conditions). Drag depends on the square of the relative speed, so it will decrease quite significantly. Lower drag means less deceleration, making life easier for the athlete.

The same logic holds for any event that includes a form of sprinting. The performance of a jump for example whether in the long jump, triple jump, high jump or pole vault, is directly related to the maximum speed that can be achieved before the leap. The greater this is the further or the higher the athlete can go. It has, for example, been estimated, that each 1m/s increase in speed in the pole vault, leads to an increase of over half a meter in the height achieved.

Many studies have been performed on the advantage gained by tailwind in various sports. The majority of those concern the most popular event in track athletics, the 100m dash. It has been estimated that an assisting wind of 2m/s improves a record by approximately 0.1s compared to that achieved in still conditions. Mureika[26] has designed a very useful web page for accurate calculations on this issue. We can use this source to examine the world record of 9.58s set by Usain Bolt.

This record was set with an assisting wind of 0.9m/s, i.e. less than half the allowed limit. If Bolt had ran with no wind at all, his "corrected" record would have been 9.62s. On the other hand, if he had been assisted by the maximum allowed 2m/s wind his performance would have been 9.53s. In this way he would have achieved an even more impressive record without actually having to run faster.

There is another element though that complicates matters further. In the last few years particular emphasis has been given to the accurate time measurement of performances that are now provided to an accuracy of 0.01s. We saw that a wind of 2m/s can offer an advantage of

---

[26] See, http://myweb.lmu.edu/jmureika/track/wind/index.html

about 0.1s. This implies that for an accuracy of 0.01s to exist in the actual performance of the athlete, the instruments (gauges) measuring airspeed must be accurate to 0.2m/s. Is this the case?

Lithorne[27] placed a series of measuring instruments along the 100m stretch of a stadium and noticed the following: First of all he observed that measurements varied across the stretch due to the presence of the stands, etc. It is also quite possible that the strength and direction of the wind can change during the 10s of the race. He reached the general conclusion that the accuracy in measurement was about 0.9m/s, much greater than the desired 0.2m/s. As we have seen, a difference of 0.9m/s in airspeed can change the athlete's time by about 0.05s. So although our stopwatch is registering with an accuracy of 0.01s, in actual fact, due to the inaccuracy in wind measurements, the accuracy is 0.05s and this for a particularly fast event.

There is a case where problematic wind measurements had almost catastrophic consequences for an athlete. That athlete was the Cuban Ivan Pedroso who in 1995 in the long jump achieved 8.96m, one centimetre further than the current world record. Although the wind gauge registered an assisting wind of 1.2m/s, within the legal limits, the record was never recognised. The reason for this was that, according to the event organisers, an official that was standing on front of the gauge was affecting the measurement results. I wonder if Pedroso and the official ever met each other to discuss the issue!

The discus paradox

There are other sports in which wind can assist a performance in ways that may have not occurred to us. Imagine that on quite a windy day you are about to take part in the discus throwing event. The games

---

[27] See the publication, Linthorne N.P., "Accuracy of wind measurements in athletics" (2000), Sports Engineering, 3, 241

official gives you the choice. Will you throw into the wind or in the opposite direction?

Most people would think that throwing into the wind would cause a greater deceleration and thus produce a smaller range. Although it may defy common sense though, this actually is the right tactic to follow. Simulations have shown that the discus, if thrown correctly, can travel for up to 5-6m further if it is thrown against the wind.

How can this be the case? The answer is provided if we think of *both* aerodynamic forces acting on the discus. Apart from the drag, which increases due to the wind presence and so has a negative impact on the performance, there is also lift which will also increase in value due to the increased relative speed. Lift is the force that keeps the discus in the air so, the more it increases, the longer the flight. By throwing the discus at the right angle the athlete can take advantage of this, thus overcoming the negative effect of drag. So apart from strength, discus throwing also requires quick thinking. On the other hand, it seems strange that strict wind limits have been imposed for events such as the 100m but not for others such as discus throwing where the effect is possibly greater.

Mexico, the favourite venue

From the drag formula, $D = 1/2 \rho S C_D V^2$, it is evident that if the air density (ρ) decreases, this will also assist a competitor. Air density decreases as we move to higher altitudes. This is the reason that Mexico City, at an altitude of 2250m, is one of the favourite destinations of athletes taking part in various events, as many impressive records have been achieved there. At 2250m the air density is about 80% of that at sea level, so air resistance will also be approximately 20% smaller.

It has actually been estimated that the world record set by Bolt in Berlin, with the same wind (0.9m/s) in Mexico City would have been 9.51s. In

Chapter 7: Are all records the same?

conclusion, if Bolt had run in Mexico City with an assisting wind of 2m/s, he would have achieved a world record of 9.46s, a truly impressive result.

A fairer comparison

So if athletes compete at different altitudes and with different winds prevailing, is there another, more just way for comparing their records? One idea would be to adjust all records to conditions of zero wind and zero altitude, in other words to estimate how fast the athlete would have run at sea level and with no wind. With the help of the website referred to previously, we can perform such an analysis for the men's 100m event.

Athlete	Time (s)	Wind (m/s)	Altitude (m)	Corrected time (s)
Usain Bolt	9.58	+0.9	34	9.62
Asafa Powell	9.74	+1.7	400	9.83
Maurice Green	9.79	+0.1	110	9.79
Donovan Bailey	9.84	+0.7	315	9.88
Leroy Burrell	9.85	+1.2	600	9.92
Carl Lewis	9.86	+1.0	10	9.91

Table 7.1 Adjusted records for the men's 100m

In the above table the records of six of the top athletes of all time are presented[28]. The sequence without taking into account wind and altitude corrections is: Usain Bolt, Asafa Powell, Maurice Green, Donovan Bailey,

---

[28] I have not included records that were subsequently deemed invalid due to the use of drugs.

Leroy Burrell, Carl Lewis. If we correct for those parameters we obtain: Usain Bolt, Maurice Green, Asafa Powell, Donovan Bailey, Carl Lewis, Leroy Burrell. The effect is quite significant. Of course Usain Bolt is still in a league of his own! An assisting wind can also work against athletes; this will be the case if an impressive record cannot be recognised. In 2008 the American Tyson Gay, ran the 100m in 9.72s, with an assisting wind of 4.1m/s. By adjusting the record to still conditions we can estimate it at 9.85s, an excellent performance, especially for that year.

As far as women are concerned, one of the most disputed world records is that of the American Florence Grifith Joyner (Flo Jo), set in 1988 (and still standing to this day) at 10.49s for the 100m event. Many researchers believe that the wind gauge, showing still conditions, was not working properly. There is some evidence that points to this. The next fastest legal times that she achieved were 10.61s and 10.62s, both with an assisting wind. Even with a strong assisting wind of 3m/s, she had only managed 10.54s, substantially higher that the world record supposedly achieved with no wind.

Let us see what Flo Jo's record would have been in still conditions (assuming of course that they were not). According to bystanders, the wind gauge used for the triple jump event (that was taking place just a few meters further down), measured a wind of 4.3m/s. If this really were the case then her "corrected" record would have been 0.2s slower, i.e. 10.69s.

Another much talked about record is that of the American Bob Beamon, who in the Olympic Games of Mexico City in 1968, jumped 8.90m in the long jump event. This performance holds the very prestigious title of the longest standing Olympic record (i.e. the best performance in Olympic Games). When it was achieved the assisting wind was exactly at the legal limit (2m/s) and the high altitude definitely also helped. So how much was Beamon assisted by those two factors? Studies have shown that the net effect was an increase in performance of about 31cm. Before this, no athlete, not even at Mexico City, had jumped more than 8.35m. Physics proves that this record was truly and objectively remarkable, and this is why it remained the world record for 23 years.

Warm velodromes

Apart from altitude, the air density is also affected by temperature. The hotter the air is, the lower the density. This is the reason that the velodrome where the London Olympic Games were held, is kept at quite a high temperature (26-28 degrees Celsius), so that the air density decreases and performances improve.

In order to study the effect of temperature on the performance of a cyclist covering 4km (this is the distance for the men's pursuit Olympic event[29]), I used the model that was presented in chapter 4. I assumed an increase in temperature of 5 degrees Celsius (from 20 to 25), which will produce a reduction in density of about 1.5%. This reduction will limit the drag acting on the athlete, increasing his speed and lowering his time. According to the very simple model, the time reduction for the 4km race will be about 1.5s. It should be mentioned that in the London Games, world records were broken for four out of the ten cycling events. Interestingly, for the men's team pursuit, the improvement was 1.636s.

The magic swimsuits

As we now know, the value of drag very much depends on the shape and the surface of the body it acts upon. In the relevant formula, these effects are represented by the drag coefficient. We have mentioned that for aerodynamic designs this number takes small values, whereas for more blunt objects the drag coefficient increases. This is the reason that cyclists wear specially designed helmets. Quite simple mathematical

---

[29] For the corresponding women's event the distance is 3km so the effect of temperature on the final time will be smaller.

calculations can prove that if we reduce drag by 25%, we can increase the speed by 10%, certainly an impressive improvement.

Probably one of the most noticed technological interventions in the field of sport had its effect on the Olympic Games of Beijing in 2008, where something remarkable occurred. In total 66 Olympic records were broken and in some events the first five athletes all broke the Olympic record! The following year in the World Championships, in Rome, the results were even more startling and no fewer than 43 world records were broken.

The reason for these impressive achievements was the use of high tech, full body, swimsuits. This type of swimsuit had already been designed in 1999, for example the *Speedo Fastskin*, which copied the design of shark skin in order to reduce drag. In 2008 the most popular one was the *Speedo LZR Racer* (see figure 7.1). Almost 90% of the medals in the Olympic Games that year were won by athletes wearing these swimsuits.

Figure 7.1: The Speedo LZR Racer[30]

---

[30] Image created by NASA (see, http://en.wikipedia.org/wiki/File:NASA_LZR_Racer.jpg#file)

Chapter 7: Are all records the same?

The special materials from which these suits were made from, reduced drag (mainly friction drag), thus enabling records to tumble. The technology used was so advanced that the project was supervised by NASA. In the end the governing body (FINA) decided that rather than having one type of swimsuit compete with the other, it would impose restrictions on all suits used in events. The records though remained valid and many predicted that they would not be broken for years. In the London Games however, despite the restrictions, new records were set, proving that the magic swimsuits were not unbeatable.

To form an idea of the swimsuit effect, we can look at the progress made in the 100m women's free style event (in an Olympic size pool). Until the year 2000 the world record stood at 54.01s. Between 2008 and 2009 the record was broken five times (four times in 2009), and reached 52.07s. The improvement in less than ten years was 3.59%. If we had a similar improvement in Bolt's world record, the 100m dash by 2019 would be run in 9.24s!

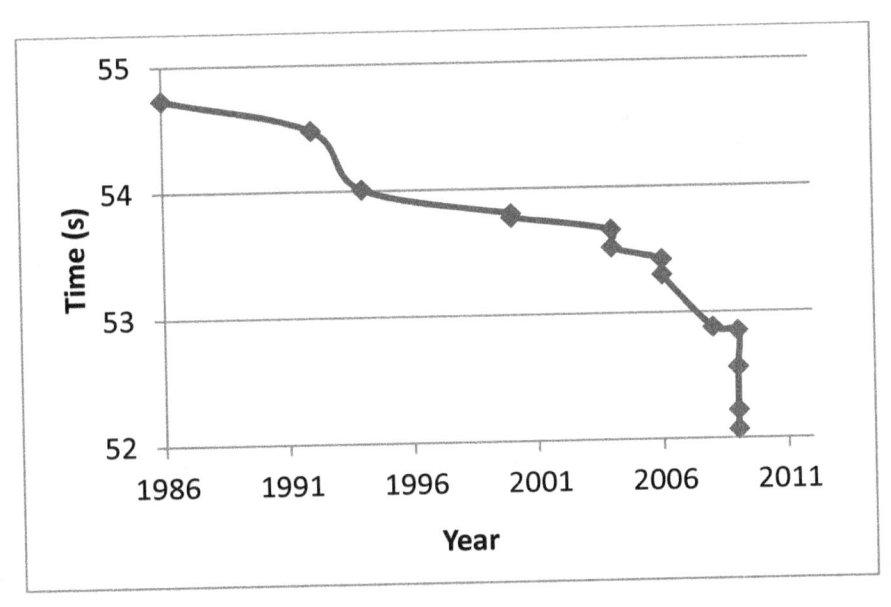

Figure 7.2: Women's 100m free style world record progress

The final whistle

At this point the journey that hopefully combines the beauty both of sport and science comes to an end. Somebody once said about football that "the ball is round, everything else is just theory". The scope of this book was to present the scientific theory behind many popular sports. A review was performed of the main physical mechanisms that define the performance of athletes. Concepts such as speed, acceleration, torque, energy and aerodynamic forces were introduced. It is hoped that the reader having become familiar with these scientific concepts, is now able to view sport with an added dimension.

General Bibliography

Armenti A., "The physics of sports" (1991), Springer
Barrow J.D., "100 Essential things you didn't know you didn't know about sport" (2012), Bodley Head
Bray K., "How to score: science and the beautiful game" (2008), Granta Books
Eastaway R. and Haigh J., "The hidden mathematics of sport" (2011), Portico Books
Goff J.E., "Gold medal physics" (2010), John Hopkins University Press
Knudson D., "Fundamentals of biomechanics" (2007), Springer
Lipsyte R. and Vizard F., "Why a curveball curves: the incredible science of sports" (2008), Hearst Communications, Inc.
Wesson J., "The science of soccer" (2002), Taylor & Francis Group

Bibliography per chapter

Chapter 1

Helene O. and Yamashita M.T., "The force Power and energy of the 100 meter sprint" (2010), Am. J. Phys. 78 (3), 307-309
Yechout T.R., Morris S.L., Bossert D.E., Hallgren W.F., "Introduction to Aircraft Flight Mechanics: Performance, Static Stability, Dynamic Stability, and Classical Feedback Control" (2003), AIAA Education Series

Blazevich A., "Sports Biomechanics: The Basics: Optimising Human Performance" (2007), A&C Black Publishers

Chapter 2

Spathopoulos V.M. "The Physics of Football" (2010), Magazine of Greek Physicists Association, "The Physical World", p. 40-44

Spathopoulos V.M., "Simulating Key Aspects of the Game of Soccer by Use of a Mathematical Model" (2009), e-journal of Science & Technology (e-JST), 4, 4, p. 57-65

Spathopoulos V.M., Nikolaou V., "Use of a Flight Mechanics Model for Sensitivity Analysis of Parameters Influencing the Trajectory of a Football" (2012), 3rd World Conference on Science and Soccer, Ghent

Fontanella J.J., "The Physics of Basketball" (2006), John Hopkins University Press

Baila, D.L., "Project: Fast ball – Hot or cold?" (1966), Science World, September 16, 10-11

Persson, J., "Measure the coefficient of restitution for sports balls" (2012), Physics Education 47 (6), 662-663

Chapter 3

Gregor, W.C. and McCoy, R.W., "Kinematic Analysis of Olympic Discus Throwers" (1985), International Journal of Sports Biomechanics, 1(2): 131-8

Hiley M.J. and Yeadon M.R., "Swinging around the high bar" (2001), Physics Education, 14-17

Kerwin D.G., Hiley M.J., "Estimation of reaction forces in high bar swinging" (2003), Sports Engineering 6, 21-30

Chapter 4

Hannas B.L. and Goff J.E., "Model of the 2003 Tour de France" (2004), American Journal of Physics, 72(5), 575-579

Haché A., "A cool sport full of physics" (2008), The Physics Teacher, Vol 46, 398-402

Stevenson R.D., Wassersug R.J., "Horsepower from a horse" (1993), Nature 364 (6434): 195

Linthorne N.P., "Energy loss in the pole vault take-off and the advantage of the flexible pole" (2000), Sports Engineering, 3, 205-218

James D., "The physics of winning - engineering the world of sport" (2008), Physics Education 43 (5), 500-505

Chapter 5

Lithorne N.P., "Throwing and jumping for maximum horizontal range" (2006), The Physics Teacher, Vol. 38

Brancazio P.J., "The physics of basketball" (1981), American Journal of Physics, Volume 49, Issue 4, 356-365

Howard A. Brody, "Tennis science for tennis players" (1987), University of Pennsylvania Press

Chapter 6

De Mestre N., "The mathematics of projectiles in sport" (1990), Australian Mathematical Society Lecture Series

Ward-Smith A.J. and Clements D., "Numerical Evaluation of the Flight Mechanics and Trajectory of a Ski Jumper" (1983), Acta Applicandae Mathematicae, Vol.1, No.3, pp. 301-314

Shinichiro I., Kazuya S., Takeshi A., "An Experimental Study on Ski Jumping Styles" (2009), Engineering of Sport 7, pp 9-17

White C., "Projectile dynamics in sport" (2010), Routledge, Taylor and Francis

Chapter 7

Linthorne N.P. and Weetman A.H.G., "Effect of run-up velocity on performance, kinematics, and energy exchanges in the pole vault" (2012), Journal of Sports Science and Medicine, 11 (2), 245-254

Linthorne N.P., "Accuracy of wind measurements in athletics" (2000), Sports Engineering, 3, 241

Pritchard W.G. and Pritchard J.K., "Mathematical models of running" (1994), American Scientist 82: 546-553

Ward-Smith A.J., "Altitude and Wind Effects on Long Jump with Particular Reference to the World Record Established by Bob Beamon" (1986), Journal of Sports Science 4, 89-99

Design of figures

The figures were designed by the author (with the Microsoft Excel© and Matlab© software), by Pany Kalkounou, and some with the help of Angelos Lakrintis.

CPSIA information can be obtained
at www.ICGtesting.com
Printed in the USA
FSHW021252301120
76442FS